203

you
deserve
healthy
love,
sis!

Also by Dr. Grace Cornish

10 Good Choices That Empower Black Women's Lives

10 Bad Choices That Ruin Black Women's Lives

Radiant Women of Color

The Fortune of Being Yourself

Think and Grow Beautiful

The Seven Steps to Getting
the Relationship You Want

you
deserve
healthy
love,
sis!

Dr. Grace Cornish

crown publishers

new york

Copyright © 2003 by Grace Cornish, Ph.D.

Published by Crown Publishers, New York, New York.
Member of the Crown Publishing Group, a division of Random House, Inc.
www.randomhouse.com

CROWN is a trademark and the Crown colophon is a registered trademark of Random House, Inc.

Printed in the United States of America

Design by Debbie Glasserman

Library of Congress Cataloging-in-Publication Data
Cornish, Grace.
You deserve healthy love, sis!: the seven steps to getting the relationship you want / by Grace Cornish.—1st ed.
1. Mate selection—Psychological aspects. 2. Love. 3. Man-woman relationships—Psychological aspects. 4. Dating (Social customs)—Psychological aspects. I. Title.
HQ801 .C726 2003
646.7'7—dc21   2002011118

ISBN 0-609-60995-5

10 9 8 7 6 5 4 3 2 1

First Edition

This is especially for you because
it's simply your time to be loved

■ acknowledgments

I have to thank God for using me as a vessel to relate this message of wholesome love. I also have to thank thousands of sisters (and brothers) throughout the country and around the globe who've trusted me with their personal stories, respected my advice, and allowed me to share some of their experiences here.

An enormous thanks to my no-nonsense literary agent, Barbara Lowenstein, who understands my work and pushes forth for me to be treated fairly. A ton of appreciation to my dynamic editorial team at Crown, Kristin Kiser and Claudia Gabel, whose keen insight, professional skills, and helpful suggestions have truly put the frosting on the cake.

As always, my immediate family, close friends, and colleagues are a big plus on my list—especially two of my dearest loves who stayed up with me many nights while I typed this manuscript: My eight-year-old daughter, Dena, who refused to go to bed until I read a few lines to her and allowed her to type a sentence or two; and my husband, Richard McDonald Livingstone, whose love, kindness, support, and healthy presence in my life had a substantial impact on the completion of this book.

And to you, for your continued support, thanks and enjoy!

■ contents

you deserve healthy love, sis!

■ introduction

a message from my soul

There is not a week that goes by that I don't receive numerous letters, e-mails, and phone calls from Black (and White) women around the country seeking help with their love lives. These sisters have already read and benefited greatly from my previous bestsellers, *10 Bad Choices That Ruin Black Women's Lives* and *10 Good Choices That Empower Black Women's Lives,* but still yearn for something more. They are seeking something extra to fill the void, to bring love into their lives and joy to their hearts. This "something more" is *You Deserve Healthy Love, Sis!: The Seven Steps to Getting the Relationship You Want.*

This is not just another relationship book—this is a tailor-made, well-crafted blueprint that will guide Black women, step by step, to achieving a better and healthier love life with a healthy-minded man. While *10 Bad Choices That Ruin Black Women's Lives* helped sisters to *face and erase* relationship problems, and *10 Good Choices That Empower Black Women's Lives* did an excellent job of showing sisters how to *embrace* self-worth, *You Deserve Healthy Love, Sis!* will take you one step further in your personal development by showing you how to make the transition from self-love to compatible love—by getting to the heart of men's motives, understanding what makes them tick, creating long-lasting relationships with them, and, more important, meeting and marrying your very own soul mate (just as I recently did).

Heck, let me be completely open here: I believe that in order to really help people make changes in their lives, I have to "walk the walk," and not just "talk the talk." One afternoon while diligently reading a pile of letters I received from some of my readers, I had to stop and pray for guidance, to ask in what manner I should answer the letters. Although each woman's story was unique, they all were dealing with one of these two common problems—being involved in a bad relationship or having no relationship at all.

And so I sighed. I sighed because I had already given sisters the tools to get out of unhealthy relationships in *10 Bad Choices,* which they had read, and admitted that it helped them greatly, yet still they were asking me for more guidance and advice on the same subject. Why?

I really wanted to know, because if they already had read the book, what more could I possibly share with sisters who were constantly struggling in their relationships? It's not that I didn't appreciate their letters—I did (and still do). But for a while I was stuck. That's why I had to pray. Then after I prayed, I thought deeply about what kind of different and unique perspective I could offer my sisters that no other book on the market could provide. I realized sisters needed something deeper—something that would not only dissolve the blockages that barred them from having decent relationships with worthy Black men, but something that would help each of them attract their individual soul mate on a higher spiritual level.

So I placed myself in each sister's shoes and asked, "What exactly is she crying out for? How could I use myself as an example—and how could it help her to heal?" With all that I had accomplished over the years, getting rid of the *bad choices,* and empowering myself with the *good choices,* there was still something missing—a connection that's nurturing, intimate, meaningful, and inspiring. What was missing, I felt, was *healthy love.* Not a needy or superficial love, but a deep, nurturing, healthy type of love. That was it! I thought *You deserve healthy love, sis!* I sure do, and so does my sister. We deserve healthy love—I and all my sisters out there looking for "something more" and "something good."

So you know what I did? I dropped everything and had a heart-to-heart talk with God and said, "I'm truly ready for this healthy love . . . and before I complete my journey on earth, I want to know and experience what it really feels like to love someone unconditionally, and to also be loved unconditionally by him *at the same time.* I am now ready for my very own soul mate." And you know what? It happened! Within the year following that soul-stirring prayer, I had three proposals, but all it takes is one person, so I chose wisely; I chose the *right* one. I can honestly tell you that I have indeed found and married my "healthy love." His name is Richard, and everything I have discovered to make this happen I am sharing with you here in these pages.

After reading this guidebook and following the seven steps, within a short period, you, too, will be writing to me to share the good news of finally getting the healthy love that you want and deserve! (Trust me, sis, if I could do this, so can you!) I am as excited for you as I was for me. Now, turn the page and let's get started. . . .

■ step 1

> **first and above,
> you must begin
> with self-love**

Sis, just for a brief moment, take a deep breath, close your eyes, clear your mind, and answer this question: What would it feel like to have someone love you just for being who you are? Someone to love you in a way that you never thought possible—a kind, generous, comfortable, yet exciting love. A love in which there is no cheating, no lies, no confusion, and no disrespect. Go deep into your feelings, sis. What would it feel like?

Does it feel strange or uncomfortable for you to imagine this type of love in your life? Do you believe it's almost impossible to meet and marry a man who will give you his best, and bring out the best in you at the same time?

Just for a moment, forget about past relationships and experiences; forget about social statistics; forget about the movies, the media, the rules, or what anyone else thinks. Right now, all that matters in your life is what you think. Whether you're presently single, divorced, or in an unfulfilling relationship, it doesn't matter; just take another deep breath, and answer this: What would it really feel like to enjoy a healthy love relationship and marriage with a wonderful man?

I am not asking you to wish or hope. I'm talking about

actually believing and seeing yourself in the healthy love relationship that you really want and deserve. Believe me, it can and will happen. I know, because it happened to me and to many other women. Everything I've learned from my research and personal experiences you're holding in your hands.

It wasn't luck or coincidence. I don't base my life on luck, nor do I believe in coincidences. I believe in blessings, proper planning, and purpose. I live by the spiritual belief that everything happens at each particular stage in our lives for a reason. We may not understand each experience at the time, but as we grow on life's path and open ourselves to God's blessings, things become more clear and more available to us.

IT'S NOT BY CHANCE THAT YOU HAVE THIS IN YOUR HANDS; IT'S SIMPLY YOUR TIME TO BE LOVED

For example, it is no coincidence that you happened to pick up this book, or that someone gave it to you, especially at this particular stage in your personal life. I believe that you have either been seeking, praying, or yearning for a different, better, or new relationship. Not just any relationship, but *the one*—the right one. The one that's right for you!

I also strongly believe in the biblical principle "Ask and it shall be given." But this is not meant to be interpreted literally. It also implies that you make a psychological and spiritual appeal. In other words, it's not solely about the words that come out of your mouth, but also about your frame of mind and behavioral pattern—your thoughts, feelings, beliefs, and actions.

Let me explain further. People may say they want one thing, yet their actions and personalities say something completely different. For example, a woman may have gone through a series of harsh and unkind experiences with men in the past, and verbally affirms that she wants an ideal mate in the present. Yet, if in fact she has not taken the time to cleanse and heal from her old memories and habits, she may, consciously or unconsciously, attract the same type of unworthy men into her life. Or, on the other hand, if a decent man steps into her life, she may not be able to bond with him in a healthy manner because past emotions will keep resurfacing and interfering with their relationship.

However, when she takes the time to first prepare herself mentally, emotionally, and spiritually, she will "ask" for and shall certainly "receive" the healthy love she seeks, and she never has to worry about ever being abandoned or lonely again.

Sis, my goal here is to help prepare you, so that you will be able to *ask for, believe in, receive,* and *accept* the wholesome relationship and marriage you deserve by first examining and then removing the hidden as well as the readily apparent emotional hindrances that may be blocking your blessings.

THE BEST PLACE TO START
IS WITH SELF-LOVE IN YOUR HEART

Each individual must undergo a self-actualization process in order to attract a soul mate on a higher spiritual level. We won't be able to find a permanent and healthy love match if we don't know how to find and love who we are first. One of the reasons so many relationships end up being bitter experiences is that the people involved did not condition themselves for better bonding. They entered into the situation prematurely. A writer friend of mine is famous for this quote: "When two half people get together, they make one whole mess."

Sis, when I decided that I really wanted a healthy relationship and happy marriage, I had to begin with self-love and go through a spiritual renewal. As soon as I was spiritually, emotionally, and mentally ready, I received the love of my life. Now it's your turn.

So the first step in this book is designed to help you create your individual healthy self-love. I will walk with you through a "Four-Phase Personal Makeover." By the end of this chapter, you will experience a fantastic spiritual renewal and will feel enthusiastic, excited, and eager to explore the following steps in this healthy-love guide.

Ready? Let's go!

PHASE 1: HEALING FROM THE BITTER FLING AND RECONDITIONING FOR THE BETTER THING

We do an excellent job of putting on a front before the world. As we step onto the threshold of puberty, the elder women within the community sing the sister-solidarity anthem: "Don't let anybody have anything over you, and never let a man know what you're really thinking."

This practice has built barricades around the hearts of countless sisters, resulting in years of celibacy, casual dating, or shallow relationships. And when we experience disappointment from unhealthy relationships, instead of exploring our emotions, we retreat even further within to an untouchable place in an attempt to bury the anger, which often leads to despondency and frustration.

We are walking around secretly tucked inside our invisible armor. On the outside, we may seem okay, but no one sees us when we are home alone at night, crying ourselves to sleep because of loneliness and feelings of abandonment. This armor successfully keeps others from getting in, but it also keeps us from getting out. We are prisoners within our own body temples.

ALL FALSE FEELINGS MUST BE EMPTIED OUT
FOR YOU TO DISCOVER WHAT REAL LOVE'S ABOUT

And it's confusing. It's confusing because armor is a sister's way of defending herself, yet on the other hand her self-protective wall is holding her captive. Many Black women have already given up on love; thousands secretly yearn for it; others desperately hope for it; and many are *afraid* to claim it.

Let's take a look at Veronica's story. Veronica, an attractive thirty-four-year-old accountant, volunteered her thoughts in one of my "Healing Black Male/Female Relationships" seminars. "Why bother?" she said to me. "I've been through enough drama in my life to keep me busy until the next century. All I wanted was one man to love me unconditionally. Was that too much to ask? *I've given up.* I have my kids, my friends, and my career to keep me occupied."

As we spoke, she ended up divulging some important revelations. "When I see couples walking hand in hand, I look the other way," she admitted. "It's not that I'm jealous, but I feel uneasy because I wish it was me. I would like someone to care about me enough to hold my hand in public, or to open a car door for me, or to just hug me and tell me everything's going to be all right."

Then I asked, with concern, "Why have you *given up?* Why don't you start dating again?"

With tears in her eyes and a tremble in her voice, Veronica confessed, "I am afraid, Dr. Grace. I've been disappointed and hurt by love so much, that I'm afraid to trust again. I don't know how to trust, so I stay away from relationships."

As our conversation progressed, I realized that she hadn't really given up on love, because she still yearned to be loved. Instead, *she had given up on herself.* In the process of removing herself from love, she had actually neglected her own feelings and desires, and buried her emotions in her "kids, friends, and career."

IN ORDER TO RENEW, "TO THINE OWN SELF THOU MUST BE TRUE"

Deep inside, Veronica was longing for healthy love with a healthy-minded mate. But the years of wearing her protective armor had created severe emotional toxic buildup. She no longer believed there was a certain someone to love her exclusively, unconditionally, and uncompromisingly. To properly prepare herself for healthy love, she had to learn how to reject toxic theories about love.

Many sisters, like Veronica, don't know where to start. They don't know how to trust, and they don't know how to remove their personal armor. The simple truth is that *the healthy love we crave must first be created within us.* Sis, you've got to let go and let the love of God flow in and through you. Replace your personal armor with the protection of God's love. Ephesians 6:13 tells us, "Take up the full armor of God, so that you will be able to stand firm." I developed the following exercise to help Veronica dissolve her personal armor. Within two weeks, she realized that it wasn't love itself that had disappointed her, it was the particular men she had been involved with. Three months later, she wrote to report that she was "happily dating."

EXERCISE: Clearing out the emotional toxic buildup

1. What was your most disappointing relationship in the past?

2. Who has caused you pain (or vice versa)? What happened?

3. How did it make you feel during that time? Why?

4. What did you want to happen in the relationship? What would you have changed?

5. Write a letter to the person (or persons) involved, and tell every detail of how you were affected (don't hold back; this is a chance to release your feelings on paper).

6. Looking back now, would you have ended the relationship earlier? If so, when and why? If no, why not?

7. How does it affect your life right now? How do you feel at this moment as you are writing?

8. Adopt this affirmation: "I, (your name), am valuable. I deserve healthy friendships, the right relationship, and a great life. I will no longer be deprived of my blessings."

9. Now, tear the letter into tiny bits, and as you tear, affirm, "I now release all painful memories from my mind, my body, my heart, and my soul. My life and my spirit are now renewed. I hold no hard feelings, and I feel no more sorrow. I am now free, and something good is about to happen to me."

10. Repeat steps 1–9 for each unhealthy relationship you can recall. (Believe me, sis, this works wonders—try it and see.)

TAKING A GLIMPSE BACKWARD
IN ORDER TO SPRINT FORWARD

Many contemporary sisters have quite a bit of toxic cleansing and self-tailoring to do because of the wear and tear caused by dysfunctional relationships with mismatched mates. There has been a major wedge driven between Black men and women since the onset of slavery and its aftermath. We mustn't dwell in the past, but we must take a look at what has caused the ruthless and disturbing behavior Black men and women often display toward each other, and move beyond these hindrances with mutual respect, kindness, and open communication.

It is quite obvious that Black men and women have been wounded, scarred, and molded by the effects of slavery and the behavioral patterns handed down from generation to generation. What's not apparent, however, is the conflict that divides them within the Black community.

This division is a result of years of accumulated misconceptions, finger-pointing, and vicious debate over who is responsible for the turbulent and despondent state of Black relationships today. This is usually followed by theories, from laypeople and professionals alike, on how the Black woman must be the glue that holds the Black relationship together because her male counterpart "doesn't need any extra stress," since he has enough trouble dealing with the "outside world" where his "manhood" is constantly being challenged and scrutinized.

PUTTING SOME "SISTORY" INTO HISTORY

I completely agree that Black men face many stressful and unjust challenges in society and should be treated with much more respect. However, I also believe it is extremely unfair that all of the relationship responsibility is continually dropped in the sister's lap. She, too, is trying to gain understanding of her "womanhood," and also attempting to find her way in life. It's time for this "divide-and-conquer" mentality to cease. Our struggles are similar. We both experience our equal share of often deplorable challenges in trying to cope and fit in with societal expectations. Yet, rarely is there discussion about the part the man must play in healing African-American relationships. Thank God, there are modern-day leading male role models, such as bestselling authors William July II, Dr. Jeff Gardère, and Bishop T. D. Jakes, who are successfully teaching and guiding brothers to becoming and sharing their very best in life, and in their relationships. Despite the few evolved men out there, women aren't operating on an equal playing field and are expected to shoulder too large a burden, at the expense of their own health and happiness.

PHASE 2: SCATTERED EMOTION DOESN'T EQUAL LOVING DEVOTION

It's time for a change on a major scale. Detrimental romances in the past have left too many sisters with broken promises, broken spirits, and broken hearts. *Sis, realize right now that you don't ever have to settle for unhealthy relationships in which you are expected to be the Band-Aid to cover your mate's wounds while neglecting your own scars.* Instead, be aware that healthy love is a balanced relationship in which both partners can be the healing balm to each other when needed.

IT'S BEST TO AVOID
THE BAND-AID BONDING

Do you know what's extremely disheartening and defeating at the same time? Due to the Band-Aid type of bonding, when a sister discovers that a man is no good for her (or even dangerous), she stifles her own feelings and still remains in the relationship, or goes back to him even after she had left him.

These women *know* that these men are emotionally unhealthy mates, and they've specifically told me so. Let's look at these two examples:

One sister, the president of a well-known national Black women's social group, told me between her heart-wrenching sobs that she was in "emotional bondage" to her disrespectful lover, who not only openly cheated on her each month with a number of her coworkers and casual acquaintances, but made her abort the baby she had been carrying for him.

Another sister, Vicki, a professional telemarketer, found out her live-in lover of two years was an undercover drug dealer who had been hiding his drugs and guns in her apartment. Seven months later, she threw him out. But here's the kicker—she didn't evict him because of his illegal and corrupt dealings—she threw him and his clothes out because his "other woman" came to her house to confront her.

She took back her keys and changed the locks, but less than three months later, she changed her mind and took him back. A year after bringing him into her home again, she admitted, "I feel like my life is caving in on me. I know he's not the type of man I want to marry. He's not a good influence for my teenage children, but I can't get him out of my system."

YOU MUST BE BOLD
TO BREAK THE STRONGHOLD

After examining Vicki's case along with several others, I found that in each situation, the woman separated from the man physically, but not emotionally. In a sense, she was locked into an emotional stronghold. She had not released him from her soul. She shared an undefinable bond with him, and that's why she gravitated back to him. And until she released him from her complete self—mind, body, and spirit—she continued to fluctuate emotionally.

It was hard for Vicki at first. But with time and proper coaching, this sister finally turned her back on her abusive suitor for good. I also helped the sister in the former example to break the chains of "emotional bondage" with the dysfunctional lover through a twofold method:

First, I brought to the attention of both sisters ten specific preprogrammed beliefs that promote fear and keep women in turbulent relationships with wrongly selected mates:

The 10 Misconceptions That Cause Emotional Deception

1. "There aren't any good men left. I might as well stick with the evil I know."
2. "No one else is going to want me."
3. "So what if he cheated; all men do. Ten percent of something is better than nothing at all."
4. "I can't make it on my own."
5. "What will everyone think?"
6. "My children need a father figure around."
7. "If I was doing what I was supposed to, he would not have done it."
8. "As long as he takes care of the bills, I better keep my mouth shut."
9. "He says he loves me and he didn't mean to do it."
10. "I want to leave, but the sex is good."

Second, I provided a useful and effective technique to help them break the negative emotional ties. This method is very important because it helps you to explore and discover exactly how someone else may be in control of how you feel about yourself. It will be much easier to disconnect from an emotionally disruptive relationship once you get a clear picture on paper of how much negative power he has over your self-value system.

> **EXERCISE: Getting the emotionally unhealthy suitor out of my system**

Set some private time aside to take this seven-point quiz. Don't just answer a quick yes or no, then jump to the next question.

Spend at least five minutes on each to work through the deep feelings and beliefs that will be attached to each of your answers.

1. Does he make me feel good about myself? Why or why not?

2. Do I feel safe with him? Why or why not?

3. Does he protect me from feeling embarrassed or unfulfilled? Why or why not?

4. Can I trust him to be faithful? Why or why not?

5. Do I feel attractive and appreciated when I'm around him? Why or why not?

6. Do I think he's a kind, caring, and honest person? Why or why not?

7. Would he be a good role model for children? Why or why not?

Conclusion: If you've answered no more often than yes, you don't have to take a second guess: *It's time to cut the emotional string with this dysfunctional and unhealthy fling!*

Here is an example of another sister who after much emotional tug-of-war was finally able to unhitch from the detrimental ties that bound her in a defeating relationship with an unworthy and mismatched mate:

Dear Dr. Cornish,

I'm writing because I'm currently in the middle of reading your book *10 Good Choices That Empower Black Women's Lives.* My current situation is that I'm a single mother of three, raising my kids alone. I was in a relationship I shouldn't have been in in the first place. I had started seeing this guy when I was thirteen; he was twenty-seven. When I turned fourteen, I found out I was pregnant. Needless to say, he left town. I had the baby, and she is now fourteen years old.

But the time in between was long and hard. Once my eldest daughter turned five, he [the child's dad] ended up back in my life. I believe my problem in letting him back in was that I was depressed, had [low] self-esteem, and wanted my daughter to know her father. From this reunion we had two more children. It wasn't an easy road. I took a lot of mental abuse in the name of "love." Had I felt better about myself, I probably wouldn't have gone back to him.

We argued over everything from money to how to raise the children. He only wanted to give me money when I would provide him [with sex]. For a while I did it because I had to feed my children. But as I got older, I started getting wiser. About five years into this relationship, I knew he wasn't the one for me. So, I started to "plot" my way out.

[The year] 1999 was the beginning of the end. . . . God started speaking to me. But I put a deaf ear to Him. It was then that my relationship with my "man" became a "threesome" (myself, God, and Chester).

I was listening to God in one ear and Chester in the other. It caused mass confusion. I could probably count on one hand the good times I had with Chester in that one year. He refused to help me in any way with the kids but I stayed anyway.

You won't progress very far
when you're involved in an emotional tug-of-war

Finally, it got to the point where I couldn't stand the sight of him. Then in the beginning of 2000, I couldn't take it anymore. I ended everything. He was mad. He called me all types of names.

A couple of weeks later, it hit me. I was scared. I was alone. Had I made a mistake? Then on the way to work one day, God spoke to me and said, "I will provide for you." At first I didn't take it seriously. I wasn't the churchgoing type, so I kind of laughed it off in my head. I guess now that I think about it, I was thinking, "What could you do for me?"

I went to Chester a few weeks later and asked him when he would see the kids. He told me to find someone else to raise my kids. I was mad. They were his kids, and because I left him, he didn't want anything to do with them.

I have to tell you about the one time I was seriously considering going back to Chester. It was in church. I had just been baptized and I was telling God [that] now things could work between me and Chester and now I knew where my priorities were, so maybe things could actually work. Well this particular Sunday we had a guest speaker. His sermon was [titled] "Don't Go Back!" I said to God, "Okay I get the message." Since then, the thought hasn't come back to mind.

I've learned that we must all go through trials and tribulations to receive our blessings. Whenever I get to the point where I feel I can't go on, I just go into my prayer closet (my bathroom) and talk to God. My house is in order. God is first in my life, and then my children. I pray every night for Chester. My hope is that one day he will open his heart back up to his children.

Just one more thing: Friends feel I should "hook up" with someone, but I am not ready. It's only been eleven months since Chester and I parted ways. It's actually been the first time in my life where I have been actually on my own. I'm taking this time—however how much it takes—to get to know me.

Sincerely,
Cora J.

THIS WILL HELP YOU DISCOVER
THE FASTEST WAY TO RECOVER

You go, sis! Cora is at a very important stage in her life. She has laid the foundation upon which she is currently building

her personal self-appreciation and self-love. Once she has
taken the time to get to know who Cora is, she will obtain a
more wholesome sense of self and will attract a more wholesome suitor into her life. You know all of us recover from
unhealthy liaisons at different paces. I have mapped out a
"12-Stage Relationship-Recovery Guideline." You can use it
as a sliding scale to determine where you are, where you'd like
to be, and how soon you'd like to get there. (Cora is currently
at stage 5.) Let's review it:

Dr. Grace's 12-Stage Relationship-Recovery Guideline

1. Recognizing that the unhealthy relationship is no good
for you
2. Conditioning yourself to get out of it
3. Taking the steps and actually walking out of it
4. Coping with the emotional roller coaster one day at
a time
5. Getting to know yourself (finding out who you are and
exactly what you want)
6. Restoring and re-creating yourself (taking back the
pieces of your spirit)
7. Empowering and enjoying the new you
8. Wanting and praying for a healthy-minded, compatible mate
9. Meeting and checking him out (letting him into the
perimeter of your life)
10. Opening to the possibilities of a new, healthy relationship as you get to know him
11. Removing your self-protective coating as you grow to
trust and respect him
12. Enjoying a healthy love match as you grow to love
each other

CLOSE THE OLD DOOR
SO THAT YOU CAN START TO RESTORE

Here's a sister who was at stage 6 when I received her letter. She decided to leave the chaos behind and, instead, take time to start anew and nurture herself so that she could be properly restored and prepared to enjoy a healthy love life.

Hello, Dr. Cornish,

While [I was] reading *10 Good Choices,* me and my boyfriend of seven and a half years were going through some problems. Although he's ten years older than me and supposed to be more mature, he's always cheated on me. I broke up with him on several occasions, but I would eventually take him back because I loved him. But not this time. After I left him, he [would] call my house or my job and I would hang up on him. Finally I got up the courage to tell him that I didn't want him anymore, not to call my house or my job, [and to] leave me alone.

In the past, I would deal with my breakups by having sex with someone else, and [then] when we [would get] back together, I, too, found it hard to be faithful. But not this time. I'm not selling myself short. I am almost thirty years old, and I have one preteen daughter. I knew that I had to be strong for her. I had to show her that it is not okay to be disrespected or cheated on. I had to show her that I can make it on my own. I pray every day to meet someone who would love me for me. Someone who will respect me and my child.

I also have difficulties with the women I work with. They make smart comments, and laugh out loud when I approach them. I have always had problems with women because of my light skin. Growing up, I had a lot of anger because the girls were often jealous, and the boys I dated were insecure, so they would often cheat on me. My daughter's father had abused

me physically, verbally, and emotionally. I was also raped
when I was a teenager; I never told anyone.

By the time I was twenty, I had been through so much. I
became defensive, argumentative, [overly] sensitive, and very
emotional. I was hiding so much inside. I would hurt people
for the hell of it. A couple of years ago, I got on my knees, and
I asked God for forgiveness, and to help me forgive those who
had hurt me, so that I could move on.

I have come a long way, and I know that I have a long way
to go. But, I will make it! I am determined to seek happiness,
joy, understanding, wisdom, and good health. I know I can't
dwell in the past. I read Psalm 105, to put the past behind me,
and move on. As for the women at my job, when I see them,
I give them a big smile, and think, *Lord, have mercy on them.*

I want to thank you for writing your books. I am going to
read them all.

> Thank you,
> Eve

SIS, NO MATTER WHAT, IT'S BEST
TO STICK TO THE HEALTHIER PATH

Eve was at a crucial turning point in her life where she realized and decided that she had to be the one to initiate the
respect and love that was due to her. I thought her letter was
a significant statement that reflected her determination to
"finally" shut out the negative drama. I could tell through her
bold declaration of "not this time" that her spirit was shout-
ing loud and clear, "NO MORE NONSENSE IN MY LIFE;
I DESERVE BETTER!"

Good for her. Here's the crucial point—although she loved
her ex, she had to learn to love herself enough to remove the
catalyst that caused her to feel unworthy, unloved, and miserable. Like most women, she wanted to experience joy and

happiness, and to bond with a good guy who could understand and appreciate her worth. She is well on her way. I knew
it took a lot of courage for her to break free from the
unhealthy and unproductive pattern of going back to the old
relationship. I was so happy for her that I had to compliment
her for starting a new and rewarding journey.

KUDOS TO YOU FOR BEGINNING ANEW

Dear Eve,

Sis, I am proud of you for saying "enough is enough." You
have now changed the course of your life, and have decided
to walk on a more peaceful and fulfilling path. You hang in
there, and keep praying for strength and guidance so that you
won't venture back to the unhealthy seven-year turbulence
that you've broken away from. Good for you for "not selling
yourself short," and instead, for holding out and seeking the
healthy love relationship that you very much want and
deserve.

I am so sorry to hear that you were raped as a teenager.
Thank you for sharing this painful secret. There are so many
women who are carrying around guilt and shame for these
horrible attacks that they were not responsible for. You are
truly remarkable; I'm so glad you were able to recognize and
break the unhealthy chain reaction that resulted from that
awful experience. You did the right thing by turning to your
faith and asking for a renewal.

Sis, you are indeed renewed. Keep on seeking "happiness,
joy, understanding, wisdom, and good health." Once you
have truly released the toxic emotional ties to your old
boyfriend, you will be primed to meet your soul mate—a special man who will love you unconditionally and also respect
both you and your daughter. Keep on the path, sis.

Yours truly,
Dr. Grace Cornish

INSIDER'S TIP: HOW TO MEND FAST
FROM A BROKEN PAST

The quickest and most effective way to move from one stage to the next in life (or love) is to analyze a person or situation from the outside looking in. People seek good advice from therapists (and friends) because the advisors are able to stand back and view the subject without personal intimidation or fearful hesitation.

The following exercise will help boost and solidify your self-appreciation and self-worth by using the "third-person" format. You will observe, develop, assess, and improve who you are by acting in the capacity of a best friend (or therapist) on the outside looking in. You'll be surprised by all the wonderful new things you'll discover about yourself.

Use a personal journal and write to your heart's content. By the time you reach the last item, you'll feel a deeper level of protection, loyalty, and kinship toward yourself. Here are the only rules: *Keep it honest, keep it real, keep it kind.*

EXERCISE: Defining my life without any strife

1. Who exactly is <u>(your name)</u>? She is . . .
2. What does she really want out of life?
3. What are her favorite colors, hobbies, movies, places to visit, topics of discussion, books, etc.?
4. What are some of her fondest and happiest memories from childhood through adulthood?
5. How does she allow people to treat her?
6. How does she secretly feel about herself?
7. What are some of her good characteristics that she would want people to know about her?
8. The things I like most about her are . . .

9. The things I would like to help her change or improve are . . .

10. She is a unique and special person because . . .

11. I believe she deserves a healthy love relationship because . . .

12. I love her because . . .

Helpful hint: Keep your journal in a safe place and periodically review and update it. I keep an ongoing one also. It is a marvelous way to help us improve our lives and live to the fullest. You can also use it for clearing out uncomfortable past memories and for creating terrific future plans.

PHASE 3: CLEARING YOUR PAST
SO THAT YOU CAN BE FREE AT LAST

I have practically lost count of the large number of sisters—from receptionists to CEOs—who have confided in me over the past two years that they have been raped, molested, or abused in their childhood. Most of these sisters are still in pain and are still seeking to empty out the tragic memories so that they can move forward and finally bring healthy and long-lasting love into their lives. It is disturbing, frightening, and tragically dehumanizing that they have had to experience and carry these ugly secrets all their lives.

Some have been forced into silence by direct threats from the perpetrators. Others have remained quiet because of feelings of shame, guilt, fear, embarrassment, isolation, uncleanness, and worthlessness. One forty-year-old sister recently broke her thirty-year silence to share this with me: "I don't know why I didn't tell anyone all these years, but for some strange reason, I felt I had to protect my father. I know he's sick, but he's still my father. Isn't that crazy? He sexually abused my five brothers and me when we were kids. I knew about all of them, but nobody said anything. We've never talked about it to this very day. I'm sure my mother knew what he was doing to us, but she said nothing, and they are still married. None of us has been able to have normal relationships. This is the first time I have ever spoken to anyone about this. I want to be able to put all of this behind me and feel like a normal person, and have a normal relationship. Will you help me?"

Yes, I will help. It's time to shatter the silence and begin healing from any disturbing secrets and tragic memories.

A SPECIAL MESSAGE FOR YOU:
IT COULDN'T TOUCH YOUR SOUL!

Sis, I prayed very intensely about what exercise I could give you to help you cleanse out and release the awful memories of being sexually assaulted. Little did I know that I would be guided in a different direction. As I prayed, these words came into my mind: *Tell her, he didn't touch her soul!*

I sat still for a little while trying to figure out what this meant. And as I meditated this message became so relevant to me: You are here today for a special reason, for a mapped-out purpose. You've been through quite a lot—a lot of awful, cruel, and hard experiences, but you made it through. You are still here. You made it through for a reason. It should never have happened to you: It wasn't your fault; it wasn't your fault; it wasn't your fault! The corrupt creature overpowered you, took advantage of you, scared you—he hurt your body; he hurt your mind; but his cowardly act *could not touch your soul!*

You see, the demonic energy that drove that individual to rape, molest, abuse, and overpower you had stolen part of your innocence; had taken many joyful years out of your life; had come to hurt and destroy you. But not anymore. You are still here because you are here for a purpose. *It couldn't touch your soul!* It has harmed your flesh, brought sorrow and fear to your mind, broken your spirit . . . but *it couldn't touch your soul!* It couldn't take you out of this world, because *you* are here for a purpose.

Today, right now, wherever you are, it's healing time! It's time to heal from the internal battle; time to heal from the external chaos; time to heal from all past memories and horrible experiences. Your soul connects you to a oneness with God. Use prayer to strengthen your resolve and help you stand firmly on a healthy path. Picture yourself being surrounded by peaceful people and pleasant places.

The waiting is over, your time has come . . . you shall never be harmed again. No energy, whether natural, supernatural, or unnatural, will have power over you. Prayer is a powerful way to uplift your soul. When you pray, go into your inner room, close your door, and open your heart to God.

GETTING FREED
FROM THE HORRENDOUS DEED

Sis, if you believe and accept all of this in your heart, I know that you will receive an awesome life-changing experience. Whatever the catastrophe that has kept you from living to the fullest and attracting the healthy love that you deserve, it is now being cast out of your way. Believe it, and you will receive it. I promise.

CASTING OUT THE CATASTROPHE

The day I received the following letter, I literally cried from my heart for this sister. I cried tears of sorrow for what she had experienced at the hands of her abusers; and then I cried tears of joy for her breakthrough and for her return to a personal relationship with God. But I didn't stop there; I prayed—I had to pray in order to quell the infuriation I felt toward the nasty creatures who called themselves servants of God but had violated this young woman. There are some truly wonderful pastors who are genuinely called by God to help in people's lives, but the particular sex offenders who molested this sister are definitely not counted among them. They need to be exposed and kicked out of their positions.

This young woman is truly amazing, because as you read her words, you'll see how in spite of the ugly circumstances she endured, she has regained her strength and is on a healthy path.

My dear beautiful sister Dr. Grace Cornish,

I am in my early twenties and recently graduated from Alabama State University, and I've been accepted into the University of Kentucky. Before I picked up your book, I felt very down, unappreciated, and had a very unhealthy personality and self-esteem. These feelings accumulated over a period of time. They came from childhood experiences (incest, molestation, gang rape, and rape by a "friend"), and many bad choices [I made as an adult].

At my home church, I was sexually harassed by both pastors, and I really lost faith in the church and eventually in God. Please keep in mind that these men were supposed to be leaders and spiritual counselors to me. On top of that mess, my relationship with my parents is weak. My father is a minister, but I don't believe he's really true to the call. He has physically and mentally abused me while my mother knew and did nothing.

My self-worth was very low. Dr. Cornish, I realize that I have a testimony to tell because I've overcome all of that. It's replaced! Thanks to you, I've given my life back to the Lord. I cannot begin to explain the changes I've observed in myself and in the way others treat me. Your book is truly a special gift from above. I was drawn to your very rewarding suggestions on the many talk shows you've appeared on. You have been and will continue to be in my prayers.

Sincerely yours and God bless,

Brandy A.

I had to contact and thank Brandy for taking the steps to take back her spirit from all those who stole pieces of it. I commended her for not being bitter, but for seeking a healthy way of living.

IT'S NEVER TOO LATE TO BE FREED AT LAST
FROM AN ILL-FATED CHILDHOOD PAST

Here's a young woman who is ready to take a detour from the unhealthy path both she and her sister have been traveling. Traumatic childhood memories of physical abuse have kept her from having relationships. To get on the healthy road, there are a couple of adjustments she must first make. However, she is ready to make a change for the better.

Hello, Dr. Grace,

I want your advice on a problem concerning my little sister. She is eighteen years old with a six-month-old baby, yet she is sleeping around. I think the problem stems from when we were little and my mother's boyfriend use to beat on all of us. I was nine years old at the time. Because of that I am afraid to date. I mostly stay to myself. My aunts are wondering if I am gay, and I am not. I am afraid of being hurt. I just get a picture of what happened when I was little and it makes me afraid.

I am still a virgin at twenty-one; meanwhile, my sister has plenty of problems. I have graduated from high school, and I am in college, but I am struggling; meanwhile, my sister quit in the ninth grade. My grandmother and aunts keep putting my mother and us down. None of them want to see us succeed. I feel if someone can do nothing but put you down, why be around them? Can you please give me some advice?

Thank you,

Pamela

YOU CAN DISSOLVE YOUR OLD SCAR
AND BECOME A NEW STAR

Dearest Pamela,

Sis, you have taken on so much in your young life—it seems as if you've been responsible for playing the roles of mother and protector to yourself, your sister, and even to your own mother, doesn't it?

It's understandable that you "are afraid to date," even at this stage in your life, because you have not yet gotten rid of the unhealthy picture formed in your childhood. Early life experiences do play a major role in shaping our outlook and choices in adulthood. And to have been caught in the middle of the dysfunctional relationship between your mother and her boyfriend at nine years old had certainly painted an unhealthy illustration in your mind of what relationships are really about.

I'm so sorry you had to be exposed to that. Please, ignore your aunts' taunting. How cruel and narrow-minded of them to try to put a false label on you because you refuse to rush into a relationship. Sis, you are doing the right thing—take your time and do not be pressured into any relationship until you feel safe and comfortable. At this point, it would be best for you to first face and erase your past experiences, and next, empower your present. Then, in the near future when you meet a really honest and supportive young man, whom you can really trust and talk to, you'll feel at ease enough to start dating. In the meantime, don't rush it. When you take the time to restore and re-create yourself, you will have and enjoy the healthy love relationship that you deserve.

I understand your personal dilemma because I have walked a parallel path, and have also gone through similar feelings and fears in the earlier portion of my life. When I was ten years old, I saw my natural mother murdered in front of me, and during my early teenage years, I never dated either. I just wasn't interested, and in the back of my mind I was afraid, and thought that I would be hurt and murdered like my mother. And, like you, I was still a virgin when I went to college, where I met my first boyfriend, who became both my fiancé and my surrogate family.

Different mind-set/Different outlet

In regard to your sister, I wish I knew a little more about her so I could give you a keener assessment. However, generally speaking, people who "sleep around" are trying to escape dealing with their true emotions and fears. Although you both experienced the same childhood trauma, you both have chosen different methods to deal with it based on your individual personalities. You are the stronger of the two, and have decided, "No one is ever going to do this to me; *I won't give in,*" so in an effort to protect yourself and "stay on the safe side," you have stayed away from all forms of relationships.

Now, your sister has the less dominant personality trait and has vowed, "No one is ever going to do this to me; *I won't get caught.*" In an effort to avoid being emotionally trapped, she keeps running from situation to situation. Her means of escaping the pain is similar to the old proverb "A rolling stone gathers no moss." Somewhere in her mind, she figures if she keeps "rolling around," she will gather no "moss"—no emotional buildup or pain. Unfortunately, this doesn't work. It's unhealthy, and eventually it is going to catch up with her.

You no longer have to bear any more fear

Both of your situations, although quite opposite, have one thing in common—both are propelled by fear. Fear is faith in reverse. Faith is positive belief; fear is negative belief. Both of you must find a healthy balance in order to gain a positive outlook on life and rewarding love relationships.

To help remove fear from your life, adopt Exodus 19:5 as personal confirmation that God is watching over you: "If you will obey my words, I will make you a special treasure among many people because all this world is mine." I believe you are a very bright and special young sister who will not take nonsense from anyone. Good for you. When you are ready, sis, I believe you will meet and choose someone just as special as you are, so that you can have the healthy love you deserve.

With love,
Dr. Grace

YOU CAN *FACE IT, ERASE IT,* AND *REPLACE IT*

Pamela needed to empty out negative childhood programming in order to have a fulfilling life in the present. The manner in which we handle situations or allow others to treat us depends on how we were treated as children. For example, in *10 Good Choices,* I shared this with my readers: "Traumatic experiences can cause us to retreat within, cutting off very important parts of ourselves from life. We will subconsciously act out our unpleasant memories because they were not corrected, just pushed aside and hidden."

Here is a powerful four-point exercise that I use in my national seminars and holistic self-help programs to help women heal from the scars of childhood and other unfavorable experiences:

EXERCISE: Removing the horrific and becoming terrific

POINT 1: *FACING IT*

Using a pencil, write in your personal journal any experience that is causing you unpleasant recollections. Be specific and include the environment, persons, and emotions involved. Record, as you write, whether you're feeling scared, angry, upset, confused, misused, abused, abandoned, etc.

POINT 2: *ERASING IT*

Examine your story. Realize that the characters in your past have no more power to hurt you in any way. Tell them how they have affected your life up to this point. Boldly let them know that you now have the power to cast them out of your life by erasing them out of your story. Using an eraser, rub them out of your journal and out of your mental environment. (You can use the erasure as a symbolic substitute to represent a spiritual clearing and wiping away of all undesirable things.)

As you do this, affirm, "I now remove you from my spiritual file cabinet. You no longer occupy any important place in my personal space. You are erased!"

POINT 3: *REPLACING IT*

Take a deep breath and a sigh of relief. Write a love letter to yourself. Talk about how strong, courageous, and special you are to have survived the past. Make bold declarations that no one has the power to ever harm you or make you afraid again. Record, believe, and memorize Luke 10:19: "Behold, I give you power over all the power of the enemy and nothing shall by any means hurt you."

POINT 4: *EMBRACING IT*

Staring at yourself in a mirror, have a heart-to-heart pep talk with your reflection: "I thank God for you. Girl, you're blessed.

You've passed through the storm, and you're not going back. You are very precious and valuable. God loves you and I love you. You deserve healthy love, sis!"

PHASE 4: A PERSONAL REVIVAL
WILL GUARANTEE A JOYFUL SURVIVAL

There is nothing more refreshing than an internal spiritual renewal. In this state, old memories and experiences will be tossed away, and your total being shall be transformed. With this kind of personal revival, you will definitely have an enjoyable survival in life and love. You will no longer be held captive by any emotional disturbances and circumstances that once had you drifting along in life, taking what was being dished out to you. You will become the writer, director, and producer of your own life's script. You shall pick and choose whom you will allow in your heart and in your personal environment.

Isn't this amazing? Spiritual renewal is personal power, sis. Personal power allows us to choose or refuse without being confused. No longer will you have to wait around for the telephone to ring, wondering, *When is he going to call?* Nor will you have to feel stuck in a miserable, drawn-out, tug-of-war relationship, fretting, "Will he ever stop cheating?"

You won't fall for any of the lies and false pledges of players who make promises such as "Honey, you light up my life; I want to buy you the moon and the stars," when actually they can't afford to even buy you a lightbulb. No, sis, not anymore. You'll tell all of the unworthy lover boys, "The Lord is my light and my salvation. I am a new creation, and I have no time to join you in careless recreation. I am now ready for my very own healthy love relationship with my exclusive soul mate, so since you're not *the one,* I will no longer let you occupy time in my personal space because your presence may block my blessings."

Whew! What a mouthful. To sum it up in a nutshell: It's time to drop the deadweight date, and get yourself the heavy-weight soul mate. You go, girl!

Let's get you spiritually recharged through a delightful fourfold process of *Dedication, Meditation, Visualization,* and *Affirmation:*

1. *Dedication* is perpetual prayer, praise, and worship. It's thanking God for everything (and even in advance); for your life, family, abundant blessings, joy, and specially selected husband. And above all for making you such a beautiful, brilliant, delightful, and dynamic treasure.

2. *Meditation* is deep, relaxed thinking. In this state you are at peace with yourself and can think clearly about exactly what you want in your life. When you meditate, set aside some personal time and find a private space where you won't be disturbed by daily chaos. Get comfortable, either sitting or lying down, and enjoy the peaceful calmness in your spirit. Think about the people, places, and things that bring you joy, and the new experiences you'd like to explore. Be at ease in your body temple, and enjoy your pleasant thoughts.

3. *Visualization* is using your imagination to form a picture of what you want to achieve. It can be described as "organized daydreaming." We create random images in our minds when we daydream, but in visualization, we tailor these images to our specific desires. For example, if you want a new car, picture yourself sitting in it and driving it.

If you want a healthy relationship, picture yourself being happily in love. I must warn you here that you cannot use this as a kind of mind control to get a certain man to fall in love with you. It won't work. All human beings have the gift of *free will* from God. So no one can spiritually control another person's mind (nor should he or she want to). What will work, however, is if you visualize yourself in a loving, fun, and peaceful environment and sense a terrific feeling of healthy love flowing all through your spirit.

4. *Affirmation* is creating through the spoken word. You can use it to program new behavior, relationships, friendships, and just about everything into your life. This technique is so powerful that ancient wisdom urges, "Be careful what you *ask for* [affirm]; you might just get it [you will]." Here's a tip that will help you to affirm healthy love into your life quickly: Don't affirm in the future tense, "I will be happy" or "I will be loved." Instead, boldly declare in the present tense, "I am *now* happy," and "I am *now* loved."

Always affirm with deep conviction, absolute intensity, and feeling. Be careful not to just reel your declarations off your tongue, or merely recite or mumble them. Believe what you're stating with all your heart. This is not just a wish, hope, or want, *it is real.* Sis, if you believe, you will receive it.

If you've completed everything in the four phases of this chapter, I'm sure you're feeling a good dose of positive self-love and you're ready to attract the healthy romantic love to go along with it.

Let's go! A great and exciting love life is awaiting you.

| check your signals
| before you wreck
| your choices

Let's face it, the traditional relationship between White women and their husbands does not apply to Black women. Many Black women have had to balance dual roles of wage earner and homemaker throughout history. They have been both the man and woman in their own lives for so long that when a potential suitor comes along, they find it difficult to let him participate in a healthy exchange in their relationship.

Life's circumstances and experiences have made many sisters so independent, strong-willed, self-sufficient, and so involved with their careers, churches, or social organizations that their behavioral pattern, either consciously or unconsciously, displays an "I don't need a man" signal.

This was the dilemma of Alma, a forty-one-year-old, never-married mother of two teenage boys. She has worked as a financial consultant in her firm for over twelve years. She holds a substantial position and earns a lucrative salary.

She had the car, the home, the job, the kids, but felt she needed "the husband" to complete "the perfect picture." When she met Patrick, a forty-year-old firefighter, she had already prepared a place for him to "fit into." Because Alma was so accustomed to running things for so long, she didn't include him in any of her decisions regarding her children, household, or social activities. At times she found herself feeling resentful and annoyed at him for interfering in her personal business.

After ten months of dating, Patrick told her that he felt there was "no room for him in her life," and he left. His revelation and departure took Alma by surprise. She wasn't aware of the signals she had sent out to him. She was living her life the only way she knew how—working, and taking care of her household.

Alma's profile is similar to thousands of modern professional Black women. She is attractive, works hard, and earns a good salary; she is intelligent, articulate, sophisticated, very personable, and wants a husband—yet she is single. Why?

MAKE SURE YOU'RE NOT TOO UPTIGHT
TO OPEN UP TO MR. RIGHT

Sis, the goal of this section is to help you to check the personal messages you may be sending, directly or indirectly, to potential suitors. It is not to criticize your independence in any way. I wouldn't dare do that. How can I rock the boat when I've been sailing in it for well over ten years myself? I am all for the independent, self-sufficient sisters. However, we can still maintain our independence without being untouchable. I used to be one of the "constantly busy, career-oriented, do-it-yourself" sisters. I was happily consumed by my work because I truly enjoyed what I did.

But about two years ago, I took a breather, lifted my head out of the paperwork, and wondered where the past ten years of my life had gone. I had helped thousands of people transform their bad relationship habits into positive practices, and there I was, too busy to take time to attract and enjoy my own healthy romance. It was time, once again, to check myself and practice what I preached.

So I decided that I wanted to share my life with a wonderful, healthy-minded, and supportive mate who loves and deserves me, and vice versa. Then, I had several heart-to-heart prayer sessions with God, but there was one in particular, a very soul-searching and tearful one, that led me to honestly check myself. I looked inward and asked myself if I was really ready to let a mate into my life, my heart, and my schedule. And after I made an agreement with myself and with Heaven, Richard, whom I had met two years before, went from being my friend to being my suitor within a month following the "big prayer."

However, when Richard and I started dating, I didn't realize that, subconsciously, I would only let him go but so far in my life. Then a couple of months into our relationship, in a compassionate and nonconfrontational way, he asked, "Honey, I'm in this for eternity, but I have to ask you an important question. Do you believe you will have time for the type of relationship we are about to create?"

"What exactly do you mean?" I responded.

"I am very supportive of your work," he explained, "and I believe that it's important that you continue doing what God has called you to do. But with everything you have on your plate, do you think you'll be able to make any room for *us*?"

BEFORE WE MOVE ONWARD, WE'VE GOTTA LOOK INWARD

Sis, I had to really stop and think. Richard was very attractive, intriguing, intelligent, supportive, and kind to me, and I really liked him. We were good for each other, and I was falling in love with the positive energy he expressed on the surface level

and from his center. I wanted to share my life with him. So I
had to unplug for a while to check my signals. But this time,
I had to have a heart-to-heart with myself—girl, I had to venture deep into my heart to remove the FRIENDS DEFINITELY,
MARRIAGE MAYBE sign that guarded the doorway to my soul. I
had to rethink all the theories and old beliefs that I'd held,
and when I felt comfortable enough, I invited Richard into
my inner world so that we could really get acquainted soul
mate to soul mate (but with no sex involved at this point—
something we had decided on together).

I am glad I did. I've since rewritten my internal sign to
read FRIENDS DEFINITELY, MARRIAGE CERTAINLY. We were
married shortly after that (I'll share more exciting details
with you in "Step 6: Making the Connection"). It is actually
lots of fun, a great relief, and very rewarding to be able to
take off the knapsack of heavy responsibilities and have
someone dependable to share the load as he helps you along
life's journey.

Sis, there is nothing wrong with allowing a boyfriend to
enter your independent world; with the right man, it is a beautiful experience. However, you have to be ready to accept his
presence on an equal level to have a healthy love. Let's examine what your signals may be telling others about you.

EXERCISE: Being independent and bold without being isolated and cold

1. How do I really feel about having to work and take care
of myself and my household all these years?

2. Am I enjoying my career, or am I just doing the work
because I have to make a living?

3. Have I ever resented a man in the past for trying to "run
my life"?

4. Is there a time when I may have turned away a potentially good relationship with a man because I was not ready to let him into my life? If so, when? What would I change about that situation today?

5. Am I open to the possibility of joint decision-making at this point in my life?

6. Am I flexible enough to learn and grow with a mate, or do I picture him in a specific role?

7. Do I feel uncomfortable when someone does something nice for me?

8. Do I feel that he will "have something over me," and I would be obligated to always return a favor for a kind deed?

9. Do I believe that I am worthy of being treated kindly? Why, or why not?

10. Am I suspicious of a man if he tries to compliment me? Why, or why not?

11. If a good man came into my life at this very moment, would I be ready to receive him? Why, or why not?

12. Do I define a man's worth by his career, position, or salary?

13. Do I view a man with a white-collar job as a more respectful, powerful, valuable, and/or suitable mate than one with a blue-collar job? Why, or why not?

14. Would I date a man whose earning power is less than mine? Why, or why not?

TO FIND HARMONY WITH YOUR HONEY, YOU'VE BOTH GOT TO AGREE ABOUT THE MONEY

Being at wit's end about earning power and money causes major turbulence in our relationships. I dedicated two chapters in *10 Bad Choices That Ruin Black Women's Lives* to this significant subject. In chapter 2, "No Money, No Honey," I d women the danger of viewing men solely as walking bank accounts, and in chapter 5, "Using Your Finance to Maintain His Romance," I warned sisters against being used by men as automatic-cash machines.

These two mistakes create ongoing havoc and unhealthy unions. In one situation, the woman takes too much; in the other, she gives too much. Both are extreme; both are damaging. The main goal in our relationship with our mate should be to create a balance—both financially and emotionally.

While researching the "money matter" in depth, I interviewed Dr. James Sniechowski ("Dr. Jim"), a nationally recognized leading authority on male issues and coauthor with his wife, Dr. Judith Sherven, of *Los Angeles Times* bestsellers *The New Intimacy: Discovering the Magic at the Heart of Your Differences; Opening to Love 365 Days a Year;* and *Be Loved for Who You Really Are.*

Dr. Grace: What is your advice for creating financial harmony, even though there may be a significant difference in earnings between both people?

Dr. Jim: Money can be the root of many relationship evils. Oftentimes, we use it as a measure of our personal value or use it against one another in belittling and demeaning ways. "If he's not making enough, he's a loser. If she's not working, she's just looking for a free ride."

When one person is making more money than the other, and that's the way it's going to be for a while, there should be a discussion of the contributions made to the relationship by the one who is making less. Both people have value; one [facet of that] happens to be financial.

It's essential during any discussion about money that the two people focus on its emotional meaning to each of them and not just talk about the numbers. That way, they can understand what power money had in each of their lives before they met, as well as what it means to them now as a married couple. Two people can hassle over numbers all day long and never reach any satisfaction because they are not dealing with the human side of money.

Money can be a demon that overwhelms a relationship. Or it can be a tool for intimacy and success. It's up to both parties to know what money means to them and to make sure their partner understands their position and feelings. Otherwise, money will become a monster that will destroy even the deepest love.

EXERCISE: How much does finance influence my romance?

1. If I had to decide between money or love when selecting a mate, which would I choose and why?

2. What does money mean to me (e.g., power, freedom, convenience, success, etc.)? How and why?

3. How do I feel about earning more than a mate?

4. Would I agree to work with him until he got his feet on the ground?

5. Would I exchange the value of other contributions for money earned? (If so, make a list of which sort—e.g., household chores, cooking, laundry, grocery shopping, balancing the checkbook, planning activities, etc.)

A DIFFERENT KIND OF DISTRIBUTION, BUT STILL
A FIFTY-FIFTY CONTRIBUTION

Sis, in order to create a healthy relationship, you must define your needs and your wants. Many times we claim that we want a certain type of man, but it's not always a healthy choice. We must, at some point, compromise (but not settle) to find a decent man. You need to seek out someone who has a nice personality and leads a balanced life. Instead of the man with the good looks, plump wallet, and nothing going on inside, select a man whom you are attracted to, of course, but more important, someone who is going to support you whether you're healthy or ill, rich or poor, young or old.

The man of your dreams should spiritually enrich your life, look out for your best interests, and sincerely like you for the individual that you are. If he does not do all three of these things, keep looking. As important as they are, money and status are not everything. Look for quality.

A lot of men may be financially endowed, yet emotionally bankrupt. That being said, a man who earns a modest living may have the most to offer you. Even if your mate makes less money than you do, it's the double income that counts these days. A useful suggestion may be to contribute on a percentage basis. For example, if you earn $62,000 and he makes $32,000, and you can both decide to put 50 percent of your salary into the household account; on the surface, your $31,000 input and his $16,000 may not be equal in terms of dollars and cents, but it is of equal value in the terms of percentage. Doesn't this seem fair? He's contributing just as much as you are—50 percent of the salary he earns.

Have you read the story of "the widow's mites" in the Bible? It describes this method of percentage contribution perfectly. Here's a synopsis: "And He sat down opposite the treasury, and began observing how the people were putting money into the treasury; and many rich people were putting in large sums. A poor widow came and put in two small copper coins, which amount to a cent. Calling His disciples to Him, He said to them, 'Truly I say to you, this poor widow put in more than all the contributors to the treasury; for they all put in out of their surplus, but she, out of her poverty, put in all she owned, all she had to live on' [Mark 12:41–44]."

FINANCIAL FUNDAMENTALS 101: "THE BIGGER THE FISH, THE MORE OIL IT TAKES TO FRY"

Sis, don't bypass a potentially good man because your present earning power may be greater than his. Look at his moral values and integrity. Let me share a very important financial secret with you: When a man makes a substantial sum of money, that usually means he has more entanglements to deal with as well. With larger salaries come larger bills, larger taxes, and larger debts. There is an old proverb that goes "The bigger the fish, the more oil it takes to fry." When you look at the underlying dynamics and work through the surface fluff, you may be surprised to discover that at the end of the day, the man with the smaller take-home pay may very well be much richer than the one with the larger paycheck. In other words, don't just look at a man's earnings; look at his debts also—how much he owes and what's left after it's paid—and, this is very important, find out what his credit report looks like. Make sure you thoroughly examine all the facts, sis.

I've done training programs throughout the United States, the Caribbean, and Europe, and I've seen too many sisters who have so much to offer but have unconsciously (and consciously) let their fear; their financial, social, or professional status; their skin coloring; their weight; or other barriers, along with other people's opinions, keep them from the healthy love they want and deserve. They are either choosing the wrong men for the wrong reasons, or using unhealthy excuses to keep themselves from choosing the right person.

1. How do I feel about contribution on a percentage basis?

2. Do I believe that this could work in my relationship? Why, or why not?

3. What are three alternatives that I believe can possibly work?

LOVE IS NOT WHAT THE GUY CAN BUY, BUT HOW MUCH HE SUPPORTS YOU WITHOUT ASKING YOU WHY

A very prominent and wealthy friend of mine, who is a naturopathic doctor, shared an honest and eye-opening story with me a few years ago. Let's call her Dr. Janice. While I was getting a checkup, we started talking about the self-esteem and relationship workshop series I was doing for a major cosmetics company at the time. Our conversation led her to reveal her own personal story. She did so with candor, great pride, and enthusiasm.

Dr. Janice: You know people look at me and say how lucky I am to be doing so well with my practice, my staff, and my family. If they only knew the half of it. It wasn't always like this. Years ago, I was a registered nurse, living on Long Island, New York, with my husband, Hubert, and three small children, ages nine, seven, and five. We had just enough to survive on with our two incomes, but with both of us working full-time, we hardly had any time to spend with our kids. I had just learned about the field of iridology (a naturopathic technique to diagnose the medical condition of the human body through the study of the iris), and wanted to study and explore natural medicine on a full-time basis. I researched, and found out that I could get certain grants to help pursue that field, but it wouldn't be enough to hire a baby-sitter to help with the kids and housework.

Hubert has always been a very supportive man. So we sat down and put all our cards on the table. I would be involved full-time and a half with my studies and work, and would barely have any time for him or the kids for about four years. We looked at all kinds of possibilities, but the best and only solution for us at the time was for Hubert to stay home and take care of our children and household full-time. He knew how important this was to me and said my happiness would make him happy. He took a gamble on me. For six years Hubert cooked, washed, cleaned, ironed, supervised home-work, read bedtime stories, and prayed with our children every night. I didn't have to worry about a thing at home. My husband was both mother and father to our kids. And when I came home, no matter how late, he had a hot meal and a warm bath waiting for me. I was able to go through school and establish my own private practice because of his decision to quit his job, give up his salary, and become a stay-at-home parent.

Dr. Grace: Wow! How did that impact your relationship?

YOU'VE GOTTA DO WHAT YOU'VE GOTTA DO, AND TUNE OUT OTHER PEOPLE'S OPINIONS, TOO!

Dr. Janice: It was an adjustment for both of us in the first six months. We were living primarily on my salary alone. But the trade-off was worth it. Our kids always had a parent at home. We had a plan, and we got the kids involved and dis-cussed it as a family. We had to go on a budget, but we stayed on track because we knew we were working toward a goal. *We* didn't have a problem with our family arrangement. But, my dear, everyone else did. My sisters, aunts, and friends, and his brothers, uncles, and cousins said all sort of things about us—from how could I let this man stay home while I was out working so hard to what kind of "weak" and "worthless" man would stay home and leech off his wife's salary.

Dr. Grace: How did you deal with that?

Dr. Janice: Sister, we ignored them. We separated ourselves from them and kept our household business to ourselves. We had enough to keep us busy by staying focused on what we were pursuing, and raising good, healthy kids at the same time.

It's funny how life works. Practically all of our family members who talked about us so badly are always coming around now—mostly to ask for loans. Some of them are even divorced and separated, and some have apologized. But Hubert and I don't hold any grudges toward them. We're too busy enjoying life.

Now we can afford to hire three full-time sitters if we need to. We have passed through some hard and trying times, but we stuck together, and were never rude to each other. We are so much more in love than we have ever been before. Our kids are all grown and doing quite well. Can you imagine if I had listened to or had gotten discouraged by the [talk of] stereotypes and the gossip about me being the only breadwinner in my household? We had a plan—and together we made it work. I still make more money than my husband, and probably always will, but we share everything together. We work together in the office, and we love together at home. Dr.

Grace, we have a good marriage. We are happy, and we are for keeps!

Well said, Dr. Janice—you go, sis!

WHAT'S MEANT FOR GOOD CAN SOMETIMES BE MISUNDERSTOOD

It is a blessing indeed to have a teammate you can work, play, and love with throughout life. But in order to get to this stage, we have to get past the acquaintance and dating stages first. Many times in the initial phases of our relationships, our intentions can be very easily misunderstood. It is painful and disappointing when you think you're putting your best foot forward, but then realize that the time and effort have all been in vain—not because the person was unkind or mean to you, but because your dialogue and the interchange you shared was not properly received. It happened to me once in the past, and I really didn't like the feeling it left me with, so I had to do something about it. Has this ever happened to you?

Here's what took place in this sister's life:

Hello, Dr. Cornish,

    I know that you receive thousands of e-mails, so I do not expect a personal reply. I just wanted to get a few things off my chest. I am a twenty-seven-year-old, single, Black woman who is really enjoying my life. I have a degree in broadcasting, but I became a flight attendant last year because I was not satisfied with my radio job. I like the work that I do now, but this will not be my career. I recently started school again so that I can earn a higher degree and become a certified sex counselor, then a sex therapist, because too many of our younger women and children are contracting HIV and dying of AIDS. I want to combine my degrees and get the safe-sex and HIV-testing message out any way I can, even if I have to do it at a public-radio station. I have been approached by some media contacts who are interested in my idea. I will finally have control and fulfillment in my career—which brings me to my point.

My friends, who are also flight attendants, are meeting these very nice Black men. They are dating, two are engaged, and my best friend just married! I am very excited about my life, and I am looking for someone who is just as excited about [his]. When I meet men, I let them tell me all of the things that they are planning for their lives, and I am happy for them because they have goals. But when I tell them what I have planned for my life, the majority of them tell me that I am doing too much for them [to get involved in a relationship with me] and that I should call them when I am not so busy.

I always make sure that I have time to myself where I can just sit and relax, and if I had someone else in my life, I would make sure to have time for him also. But no one seems to want to stick around for that. I just don't understand why I can't find someone who wants to be with a woman who wants to do even more with her life. Yet those of my friends who are very happy with their chosen career seem to have no problems finding men who want to commit to them.

I must say that when the terrorist attacks happened on September 11 [2001], the Lord showed me how many people cared for me because I have never received so many phone calls in my life from family and friends who wanted to make sure that I was safe. But it did hurt me a little when my girl-friends were telling me how concerned their boyfriends and fiancés were—calling them all day because they were so worried about them.

Could you tell me if I am doing something wrong? Should I not tell them what I want to do with my life? Any advice you could offer would be greatly appreciated.

Thank you,
Wanda J.

DON'T GIVE UP YOUR LIFE TO BECOME A WIFE,
BUT READJUST YOUR PACE TO CREATE SOME SPACE

My dear sister Wanda,

First, let me congratulate you on your ambition and chosen profession. Yes, I do get quite a heavy load of letters, but with the help of a supportive staff, I try to answer as many as humanly possible. I think it's wonderful that you have such a positive drive to help so many women and children to avoid and/or deal with the AIDS epidemic that is robbing the world of too many lives. You are indeed a remarkable sister.

I don't believe you are doing anything wrong in sharing your dreams, aspirations, and goals with the men you meet. However, from your letter, I gather that it has happened on a few occasions that once you've revealed your future plans to them, "they don't want to stick around."

There could be several reasons for this, but here are two main probabilities:

1. Either the men that you are meeting are somewhat self-centered, insecure, or intimidated by an upwardly mobile woman.

2. Or, maybe, you're being misunderstood and sending out the wrong signals, not by what you say, but by *how* you say it.

Since these guys appear to be "very nice Black men," and these disappearances have happened several times, I don't believe it's your future profession that might be scaring them off, but rather the amount of information that you give them, the manner in which you give it to them, and the time in which you choose to share it with them. Do you usually tell them everything at once on the first date, or do you wait until the second or third? Do you spend time getting to know about each other's personality before you talk about each other's profession? How is your voice tone and modulation during these conversations?

Now, sis, you have to really think about this one, and answer it honestly: Do you really listen and pay attention to what they share with you? Or do you come across as just "waiting for your turn to speak" and having too much on your plate?

The reason I am bringing forth these questions and cautioning you to check your signals is because you stated that they have all said that you should "call them when you are not so busy." Think back on your conversations and try to pay attention to the messages you may have sent off, because as beautiful as your intentions were, they were being misread. You also shared that you always take time for yourself and would make time for your future mate, too, but, very unfortunately, the brothers missed this very important and vital point. They were not able to "read between the lines," and did not get that message from your conversations. Sis, do you see where I'm going with this?

You've got to make room if you really want a groom

I believe that they interpreted you as having it all mapped out with no room for them in your life. Men want to feel needed, even if it's just to screw in a lightbulb. I'm very proud of you for being independent and on the move. But I also want you to get the healthy relationship that you want *and deserve.*

In response to your observation that your flight attendant friends are meeting and dating very nice Black men, let me share with you what Margaret Kent, author of the *New York Times* bestseller *How to Marry the Man of Your Choice* wrote: "Three traditionally female occupations facilitate marriage. The airline hostess [flight attendant], the waitress, and the nurse succeed with men because they portray approachability, friendliness, and concern with the man's comfort. Men view this effort and attention as an indication that they are liked, and these women therefore have access to men in all social strata."

Thank goodness, for clarity's sake, she added, "You don't need a traditional occupation to meet and marry the man of your choice. In fact, you may do far better in meeting men if your occupation is nontraditional."

I believe that you can meet the right man anywhere, anytime, and in any occupation. Still, the most important thing is what underlying messages you may be sending him. Your signals can either attract him and lock his attention onto you like a guided missile minus the danger, or it can repel him and have him running for the nearest exit. Sis, just take the time to answer the questions I posed to you; be yourself, but adjust your signals, and, most important, pray and give God thanks in advance for matching you with your soul mate.

By the way, I am glad that you are okay and did not get hurt by the terrorist attacks on 9/11/2001. I am going to be just as happy for you when you write to me to tell me that you've checked your personal signals and have attracted the loving, supportive, compatible, and *right* man for you.

Go for it!

Dr. Grace Cornish-Livingstone

CLEANING THE SLATE AND OPENING THE GATE

After receiving my response, Wanda followed up with an e-mail and remarked that she hadn't realized that her intentions were being misunderstood and that she appreciated receiving guidance to help her explore her method of communicating with men. She wrote, "I will print the questions that you have sent me, and I will seriously sit and think about how I come across to men. I have never thought about the things you have brought to my attention. I automatically assumed that it was the men I was meeting and never thought about checking myself. This will be an excellent way to start the New Year. Once again, thank you for responding to my letter and for your wonderful advice. I will let you know how things work out for me."

Sis, in order to move on to the next step on your path to healthy love, you have to make sure that you are ready for the new, terrific, and enticing experience by examining and readjusting all the misunderstood indicators in your life. The following exercise will prove to be helpful:

EXERCISE: How do my signals impact who I attract?

1. Are there any personal signals that have hindered me in past relationships? If so, what are they?

2. Do I feel that men sometimes misunderstand my good intentions?

3. Are there any specific situations that I would like to act over in my life? If so, what are they? What would I change? What would I do or say differently?

4. Do I believe that men are intimidated by me? Why, or why not?

5. Do I feel that Black women are superior to Black men? Or vice versa? Or do I believe we are equal?

6. Do I respect Black men; do I really care how they feel? Why, or why not?

7. Do I compete, or have I ever competed, with a potential mate's accomplishments?

8. Do I feel I can be forthright and feminine at the same time? Why, or why not?

9. Do I feel I have to try to impress men with my brains and aspirations in order for them to like me? Explain why.

10. Am I who I want to be?

A TIME FOR READJUSTING: NO MORE SIGNALS
THAT ARE MISTRUSTING

This sister took the time to take an honest look at what she didn't like, mapped out who she wanted to become and whom she wanted to attract, and went for it.

Dear Dr. Grace Cornish,

Let me tell you about myself. I have a master's degree, and I am a manager in the firm where I work. I also just started as a college professor, and my two teenage daughters are doing fine. I am the woman you probably would call the successful career woman, but I have made many bad choices when it comes to dating Black men.

Until recently, I saw myself in some patterns of *10 Bad Choices That Ruin Black Women's Lives.* I have "looked for Mr. Right in the wrong places." I listened to the corny lines and I believed them. I have also "exchanged sexual dealings for loving feelings." It took me a long time to realize that just because I give up sex that doesn't mean the man will love me.

When I was nineteen I hopped up and got married. We had sex on the first date, and then ten months later I saw myself walking down the aisle. Seven years later I had two beautiful daughters, but a man who was only focused on himself. I never got to develop a friendship with him because sex hid a lot of the issues.

The marriage lasted for seven years, and [then] we divorced. I became a single mom, developing skills to become a career woman and a devoted mother. After my divorce, I had to bump my head a couple of times to realize that sex doesn't equal love.

I have also stayed in relationships with men even though the respect was gone. I had to come to grips with myself and [be] a good example for my daughters. I wanted them to

ҽ [healthy] choices when they got old enough to start dat-
I have come to realize that I must make good choices.

Deleting the old mess and becoming my new best

First, I had to look at my past mistakes and see where I
went wrong. I had to look at myself, and this is what I realized: I needed to develop a healthy self-love. What I did was
hug myself and said out loud, "I'm beautiful, I love me, I
believe in me, and I want a decent man to come into my life."
I needed to not only say these words, but needed to *believe*
what I was saying.

I knew by doing this that I would only accept good choices.
I then looked into myself deeply to see if I was ready for a
commitment. I went and wrote ten good things about me and
ten things that I need to improve on. This has been taped on
my refrigerator for the past six months. I look at my list every
day to see if I'm on the right track. What really helps me is to
read daily Bible passages, and I walk three to four times a
week. I also pray all the time and ask God for His guidance.

One of the turning points in my life was when my mother
passed away last summer. A couple of days later, I was in a
bad car accident, and the car was totally wrecked. I was not
injured at all. That could have only been God's arm wrapped
around me. My daughters and I became closer, and I knew
there was a purpose for me to be alive.

Every day, remember to say, "Thank you, Lord; healthy love is coming my way!"

Last Christmas, my youngest daughter and I went to feed
the homeless. There was joy in my heart, and I loved helping
[the] children and the adults with their plates. A couple of
hours passed by, and this man came up to me. His words
were "I know you have been blessed, and you look so happy."
This man, Samuel, was also there volunteering. We talked for

about thirty minutes, and then we exchanged phone numbers. We have been dating, and we have not had sexual intercourse. We are developing a friendship, and we are both taking it slow.

I do believe my blessings are waiting for me, and thank you so much for being my mentor and for your help.

Sincerely,
Lynne A.

This sister is on a fantastic path. You can feel the joy, love, and laughter dancing in her words. Sis, the waiting is over. The time is *now* to meet, unmask, communicate, and choose healthy love in your life. Go for it!

don't be fooled—
read him well and
remove the mask

Sis, wouldn't you like to be a "fly on the wall" and eavesdrop in order to get the scoop on what *really* goes on in men's heads, hearts, and discussion groups?

Well, rest assured, I have done the work for you!

This chapter will answer a lot of questions for the wide range of women I frequently encounter in my travels, seminars, private practice, and on TV and radio talk shows, who ask, "What happened? He was so nice in the beginning, then he just changed. Why?" And not only why, but *how*? *How* can they avoid being caught up in Mary's dilemma?

DON'T BE ANOTHER TO BE KNOCKED DOWN
BY THIS HIT-'N'-RUN BROTHER

What Mary liked most about Lawrence was his keen interest in and admiration for her. While other men in her past had displayed a PROCEED WITH CAUTION sign around their necks when it came to commitment, Lawrence engaged in a full-speed-ahead chase. Within the first hour of their conversation, he asked her where she had been all his life. How soon could he see her again? Could he take her away for the weekend? Would she allow him to put her on a pedestal?

She was flattered, but felt a bit uneasy. However, her apprehension began to dissolve as he continued to shower her with roses, cards, poetry, and daily messages on her answering machine. She could not remember when she felt so special or attractive. His sweet words and thunderbolt persistence made her believe that her initial hesitance was unnecessary and somewhat childish. The self-protective coating around her heart was rapidly melting away as she began to yield to his ongoing promises of a life filled with great sex, fancy restaurants, and fun trips. It was up to her, he insisted, to give the green light for him to be her protector and provider for life.

Finally, after three weeks of Lawrence's pressing pursuit, Mary tossed away her caution and her clothes, and shared a blissful night of intense passion and climactic sex that left her feeling giddy with delight.

"I feel so special," she confided. "You are incredible." Lawrence smiled approvingly, hugged her gently, kissed her tenderly, got dressed rapidly, and assured her he would call later.

"Later," however, never came.

IT HURTS TO GET THE *LATER* FROM THE SMOOTH OPERATOR

When Mary did not hear from Lawrence after their close encounter, she was devastated. Had he been in a bad accident? Was he okay? Did an emergency come up? Did he get fired? Did he leave town? Should she call the police? She was worried sick. She called his home, beeper, and cell-phone numbers, but got no response.

She wanted to call his job, a family member, or a friend, but realized he hadn't given her any of those numbers. After three days of hysteria, not knowing if he was dead or alive, she managed to get him at 10 P.M. on his home phone. "I have company right now," he said in a cool detached tone. "I can't talk now. Uh . . . I'll call you later."

What went wrong? Was it something she did or said that sent him running? Mary, heartbroken and confused, was rehearsing and analyzing every detail of their three-week romance. Hadn't he promised to love her always? Wasn't this the same man who promised, only three days ago, that he would protect her for life? Had he changed his mind because of her performance in bed?

Wasn't I good or pretty enough? she wondered. *What did I do to turn him off?* Mary decided Lawrence retreated because she wasn't good enough for him. She began to sabotage and criticize her self-image. Maybe it was her nose, her thighs, her butt, her breasts, or her shape that turned him off, for didn't he adore her until she got naked for him? What was wrong with her?

There was nothing physically wrong with Mary, but something was fundamentally wrong with her actions. She carelessly misused her heart, instead of wisely using her head to take her time to get to know Lawrence's true intentions before developing deep feelings for him. In other words, she failed to unmask him before she undressed him. This is one of those hellish dilemmas you wish was only a bad dream that would be interrupted by the sound of your alarm clock in the morning. But unfortunately, Mary had the rude awakening of being caught off guard by an unworthy masked manipulator.

However, it was Mary's responsibility to protect her body temple, her sexuality, and her emotions. She gave up sex too quickly, too easily, and too freely. Mary admitted that she felt "uneasy" about Lawrence's desperate come-on, but she ignored her intuition and discerning spirit that were warning her, primarily because she was blinded and misled by the mask covering his true intentions.

EXERCISE: Take an intuitive look to avoid his deceptive hook

1. Do I throw caution to the wind, or do I proceed with caution in relationships? Why, or why not?

2. Do I pay attention to the facts and read between the lines, or do I only listen to what I want to hear?

3. Have I ever gotten a hunch that he might already be committed or married, and ignored my feelings?

4. Have I ever felt that it was too soon to have sex, but I did it anyway? When, and why?

5. Do I remember seeing flashes of him as being abusive, a wild playboy, or a seasoned freeloader and dismissed my thoughts as being childish or paranoid? When, and why?

6. Have a man's actions ever spoken to me louder than his words, but I went for the words instead and regretted it later? When, and why?

THE BEST WAY TO ENTER IS TO ANALYZE HIS CENTER

Wouldn't it be a great relief to be able to identify the true intentions of the men we encounter in our lives, before embracing them into our hearts?

I've done the groundwork for you. This important information will help you to detect and decipher the true motives behind a potential mate's intentions. The wisdom of the best experts on men—the men themselves—will give sisters "insider's secrets" on how to see beyond the masks of potential suitors. I have gathered the information from leading male experts, who have directly interviewed thousands of Black men around the country, in order to answer some of the most pressing and heartfelt questions I have received through letters and phone calls from my readers.

The research I share with you will be a very important step toward healing the conflict and turmoil between Black men and women. Not only will it help us to open up and communicate with each other, it will also help us to understand the hows and whys of our behavioral patterns toward each other; and lastly, help us to remove the destructive barriers that have kept us from treating each other with compassion and kindness.

Some of the questions that I will ask the male experts in the "Removing the Masks" sessions are similar to those women have asked for years—in beauty parlors, women's support groups, slumber parties, and social clubs—but still have not found the answers to. One of the most common questions is "How could a man love more than one woman at the same time?" The second part to this question is usually "Could it be true love, or is it that he loves one woman entirely, but loves certain things about the other?"

The reason sisters have not found answers is that they have been asking other women instead of directing the inquiries directly to the source—the men. If you want to find out about any subject—be it math, money or men—you have to study that particular subject.

REALITY CHECK: THERE ARE MANY MEN WHO RETREAT FROM BEING A CHEAT

The study sessions in this chapter will help you to peel away layers of deception and misconception between African-American men and women. Let me explain: It will help women to spot the deceptions of the Black men who cheat, *but it will also help women to deal with their own misconceptions that all Black men are unfaithful.*

For instance, some years ago, when I wanted to find out if the popular belief that all men cheated was true, I held an informal study session, headed by my own father. When I presented the question, my dad looked at me with deep concern, and after a brief pause, he looked me right in the eyes and answered honestly, "Grace, not all men are unfaithful. There are some very good men who would never think of cheating on their wives. Many of my close friends are among them. There are basically four types of men:

Some cheat when they are younger, and stop when they get older.
Some don't cheat when they are younger, but start when they get older.
Some never stop; *but some never start."*

Wow! This was both a revelation and confirmation for me. Not to mention what a relief it was to hear from a man who admitted to have cheated in the past, that *"not* all men cheated." It was certainly refreshing to get an honest view that counteracted some of the stereotypical and widely accepted jargon we believed about Black men and infidelity.

SESSION 1: REMOVING THE INFIDELITY MASK: "IT'S A DEFEAT TO STAY WITH A CHEAT"

To get deeper into the heads and hearts of men and their issues and feelings, who better to turn to than William July II, one of my good friends and author of three national bestselling books, *Brothers, Lust, and Love; Understanding the Tin Man;* and *The Hidden Lover.*

Dr. Grace: William, you are widely respected as one of the leading experts on male issues across the country. You have interviewed and touched the lives of thousands of men (and women) over the years. I am going to get straight to the point with this two-part question that sisters want to know the answer to from a male's viewpoint:

    a. How can a man love more than one woman at a time?

    b. Could it be true love, or is it that he loves one woman and certain things about the other?

William: Dr. Grace, this question calls for straightforward honesty. You came to the right place for the answer. Before delving into this, we must first make sure everyone is on the same page when it comes to the meaning of the word *love.* I take it to mean the "deepest affection, honor, and respect a person can have for another person." Implicit in this definition is the idea that when one loves a person, [one] focuses all of [one's] romantic and erotic energy into that particular relationship.

Therein we find the answer to the question. Love is ultimately about achieving the highest possible degree of affection for another person. While a man can experience a deep affection for more than one woman at a time, he can ultimately only have one number one love at a time. Let me say that again. A man can only have one woman in his life who is his number one love at a given time. Why? This is because love is an achievement of the highest and deepest level of affection, honor, and respect. You can't split that kind of energy up into parts and put a little here and a little there. If a man is doing that, then what each woman really has is only a piece of him, not his actual "love." Those pieces of himself he shares can be deeply affectionate places in his heart. But it's the same as having a third of a pie instead of the whole thing. Therefore, it's far less than sharing a fully functional loving relationship.

A MAN CANNOT SPLIT REAL LOVE INTO DIFFERENT PIECES WITH DIFFERENT WOMEN

William: I hear men talking all the time about how they "love" this woman and how they also "love" another woman, or three . . . or four . . . or five! But the reality is that if we were to break it down and look closely at what these men are really saying, they're not really talking so much about love, but something else. Men who say they are in love with more than one woman usually love something in particular about each woman, but don't love her as a whole person. They may love one woman's looks. They may love another woman's soothing personality. Another woman they love because she's exciting, while there's a woman on the other side of town whom they love having sex with. None of those situations are actually love. They're admiration, deep affection, amusement, or lust, but those things aren't the same as love. When you love someone, you dedicate all of yourself, not just a piece. Likewise, when you love someone, you accept them in their wholeness; you don't just take a piece. *Love* is a highly misunderstood and misused four-letter word.

SESSION 2: REMOVING THE INTIMACY MASK: "WE CAN TALK ABOUT SEX WITHOUT GETTING VEXED"

Next, I interviewed Dr. George Edmond Smith, a board-certified family-practice physician and author of *More Than*

Sex: Reinventing the Black Male Image, to talk about the making of a monogamous relationship. Here's a portion of our interview:

Dr. Grace: It is no secret that a lot of Black women believe that Black men are afraid of making a monogamous commitment, which is based on the sisters' past experiences and societal conditioning. Why do you think this belief is so widespread and popular today?

Dr. George: There is a major discrepancy about what Black men and women want in relationships. This is not about bashing one or the other, but understanding each other. Black men say [Black] women don't appreciate them, and Black women say Black men don't cherish them. They are having a hard time understanding each other. This is because we have bought into the myths and stereotypes that state what a "man" should and should not do. The biggest myth of all is that "all men cheat." This is not true.

In our society, Black men are defined by their sexuality, and this is unfair. . . . I found out that machismo and sexuality alone were not enough to support long-term relationships. I had to develop other aspects of my personality. I was lacking the emotional and spiritual aspects. Over the years, I had to learn to see women as equal beings. Sex alone wasn't enough. I had to reinvent and redefine myself first, so that I could effectively help other Black men (and women).

HOW CAN A MAN WITH A POLYGAMOUS PAST BECOME ONE WHO'S MONOGAMOUS AT LAST?

Dr. Grace: We really need to build healthy relationships that will lead to building healthy families, and healthy communities. My dad is a good father, but in the past, he had not been a saint in his relationships. He does give me excellent advice about men in general and has assured me that *not* all men cheat.

What I got from his words of wisdom is that we have to view each man on an individual basis. In your opinion, what would make the men who cheat become more monogamous in relationships?

Dr. George: They have to feel that having the relationship is top priority, and value it as a long-term one. There is a lot of moral decadence and decay in society, and we have digested it in our households. We must begin to regroup. Our race is in jeopardy. I hope to give [Black] men a wake-up call. We have to let people know we need to save the Black family. We must begin by maintaining long-term intimate relationships. Men need to become more God-based. This way they will enter into relationships without fear of being too "sensitive" or "soft." This will eliminate a lot of the verbal and physical abuse, and also a lot of the anger and domestic violence.

YOUR BEST DEFENSE: SAY NO TO NONSENSE
AND ALL FORMS OF VIOLENCE!

Dr. Grace: Both my mother and my aunt were murdered by Black men who refused to let them go, and decided to kill them instead. That was very painful for me, but I haven't allowed myself to become bitter toward Black men. As a matter of fact, due to those awful experiences, I am more on a mission to create healthy relationships between Black men and women so that no one else has to suffer like my family has.

From a male's and from a doctor's perspective, what do you think is the cause of domestic violence and brutal beatings?

The latest statistic reflects that a woman is beaten every twelve seconds across America.

Dr. George: I have witnessed my father beat my mother, and the police would come, and blood would be all over the place. To understand this violence, we have to go back to "trait and disposition" psychology. People are born with certain traits and dispositions. In our society, the physical self has had more value than anything else. Domestic abuse comes out of the unhealthy physical self. Now, if you add racism, and the cultural and social disposition to the mix, this individual is not capable of seeing beyond aggressiveness.

When men with off-balanced dispositions feel that their manhood is challenged, or feel less than a man, the rage comes out in physical anger. The anger is acted out in violence. They act on a primal animalistic plane. To heal this, we must stop reading the foolish novels about "how to be a player." We need, as a people, to begin reading self-help books, the Bible, and empowering books that can help us survive.

THE HEALTHY FIX IS TO GET GOD IN THE MIX

Dr. Grace: I agree wholeheartedly. What's your advice to our sisters for forming healthy relationships with healthy-minded men?

Dr. George: Make sure the man is God-based. He doesn't have to be a devoutly religious man, but a man who respects and fears God, whether he happens to go to church or not. Communication is a major key. You have to feel comfortable with each other.

Dr. Grace: Dr. George, let's break this down, and target how to make the coupling in relationships work. What would you say is the most important ingredient?

Dr. George: Honest communication. For instance, one of my patients did not tell his wife that he couldn't have an erection in the last three months. So he avoided intimacy with her. She thought he was having an affair with someone else. He felt if he had told her, she would see him as less than a man. After examining him, I found out this problem existed because his blood sugar was low.

The lack of honest communication could have cost him his marriage. Man is not defined by sex alone; not by how many women he can bed, nor by how many orgasms he has. He is a [complex] human being.

Dr. Grace: Well said. I must add two more important factors to the honest communication—a good sense of humor and good hygiene are also important ingredients in building healthy unions. Thanks, Dr. George, for sharing your insight.

SESSION 3: REMOVING THE COMPLEXION-COMPLEX MASK: SIS, YOU CAN WIN WITH ANY COLOR OF SKIN

While formulating the research contents for this book, I was listening to one of the most popular radio talk shows on WLIB-AM in New York called *Hit It!* The discussion of the day focused on the trend of Black women who used bleaching cream to lighten their skin color in hopes of appearing more appealing to Black men. The phone rang off the hook as Black men and women called in to give their input about

the complexion complex within the Black race and how it affects our relationships.

In regard to the color issue, some were frustrated, some were very angry, but many were relieved that it was finally being discussed openly. Sis, I tell you this, it was only an hour-long show, but the ongoing interest and discussion could have easily created a three-hour program. I was very impressed with the expertise of the host, clinical psychologist Dr. Jeff Gardère, coauthor, with Montel Williams, of *Practical Parenting,* and also a friend of mine.

Dr. Jeff, founder and director of Rainbow Psychological Services (in Brooklyn, New York), is also a nationally known TV–talk show mental-health expert, who helps and interviews hundreds of men for his ongoing research and private practice. Because of his vast knowledge, I have invited him to share the male perspective of how the color issue affects our lives and our relationships.

Dr. Grace: Dr. Jeff, why do you think the shades of people's complexions are still such a controversial issue in our race and relationships today?

Dr. Jeff: Because we do not address the subject properly. Many feel as if it's an issue of the past and should be swept under the rug. They feel it's not a problem. Some feel if they ignore the situation, it will somehow disappear. But as you know, Dr. Grace, life doesn't work that way. We all need to share the responsibility to be honest about this issue so [that] we can be free from it, instead of pretending it doesn't exist.

TURNING "DIRTY LAUNDRY" INTO "CLEAN LINEN"

Dr. Grace: So true. In chapter 1 of *10 Good Choices,* "Embracing the Skin You're In," I addressed the color com-

plex in our race and how it can damage our sense of worth, both individually and collectively. You are right on target, Dr. Jeff, because the only way to erase this type of false programming is to acknowledge it, analyze it, and abandon it. What's your advice for getting beyond this point?

Dr. Jeff: We have to air the dirty laundry. We each have to start from where we stand and admit we have a problem. We must admit that racism plays a large role in this, and break out of the box. I have to emphasize once more that we each must take the responsibility to first examine our own belief, then bring it to the table and expose it. We have to stop covering up—that does more harm than good.

Dr. Grace: You know, I use this analogy in all my books and seminars based on my "Face It, Erase it, Replace It" program: If you have a wound on your foot and do not treat it, doesn't the affliction become widespread? If you bandage it, cover it up, because you are ashamed of "John Doe" seeing it, won't the disease continue to fester, until you eventually lose your foot? But if the wound is exposed and properly treated, so what if John saw it? Wouldn't it be better if he saw it, and it healed?

Dr. Jeff: Great analogy!

IT'S NOT THE SKIN TONE, BUT WHAT'S IN-GROWN THAT WILL INFLUENCE HEALTHY ROMANCES

Dr. Grace: How do you feel the complexion complex affects relationships between Black men and women?

Dr. Jeff: I think that quite often we let skin color dictate our judgment about whom we should date. I feel because of skin tones and certain social circles, we may choose to get involved with a lighter-skinned person—that particular individual may not be nice, but we are blinded by false standards.

However, this seems to be happening less and less. As a matter of fact, many light-skinned Blacks are being ostracized because light is supposedly not "in" right now. Many light-skinned Black men like myself are not considered the in thing. Some Black women will only date dark-skinned Black men because they say they love the beauty of their skin; others say they will only have babies by dark-skinned brothers because they don't want to thin out their blood. And many light-skinned Black men only date women with beautiful dark skin.

Dr. Grace: It seems as if the trend is going from one extreme to the other—what we need to find is balance in our race. I personally have always loved my beautiful dark complexion, but I've also admired and appreciated the many different skin tones of my sisters and brothers within the Black race, ranging from blue-black to porcelain-beige. We, men and women alike, need to appreciate who we are, and respect what the Creator has blessed us with.

Dr. Jeff, in closing, will you give some advice on what makes a relationship work?

YOUR LOVE WILL GLISTEN AS YOU LEARN HOW TO LISTEN

Dr. Jeff: As you know, Dr. Grace, it's all about communication. You have to grow together—learn to trust one another—learn to lean on each other. Your mate must be your friend, your confidant, your support. *You must learn to speak, and learn to listen.*

Also learn how to be intimate. A lot of people know how

to "screw" and how to be there physically, but they don't know how to make love and be there emotionally. Communication is the key. I didn't learn that until my seventh year of marriage, and I've only been married seven years. It was six years of hell. But last year, we worked through it all and learned how to finally communicate, and now we have a good marriage.

Dr. Grace: Wow, you are so honest. I admire that. Are you sure you want me to include the part about your marriage in this interview?

Dr. Jeff: Sure I do. Like you, I believe in being open and to the point. How else are we going to help people [with their] lives? I went through a tough test, and I've passed because now my marriage is good, but we had to work on it together.

Dr. Grace: No wonder you're such a big hit. You certainly have "walked the walk" and now you can honestly "talk the talk." You go, Dr. Jeff! Thank you so much for being a guide for so many lives, and for being a positive role model for hundreds of Black men. Keep up the good work.

DO YOUR LOOKS HAVE AN IMPACT IN KEEPING YOUR LOVE INTACT?

It's a given that men love beautiful women. But what exactly is their perception of beauty, and how does it affect our relationships? The individual answer depends on the individual man. Different men have different preferences.

The beauty issue is such a pressing subject in our society, and seems to be magnified within the Black community. Due to social pressures, sisters try their best to adjust and contort their appearances to capture the attention of the opposite sex. Their assessment is based on the information provided by advertisers, who usually bombard us with images of what men desire, and what is considered "the ultimate beauty." Unfortunately, their perception of the ultimate beauty can only be attained by a minute section of the population who resemble pinup girls parading on the cover of magazines such as *Sports Illustrated* or *Playboy.*

It seems that the vast majority of these magazines have forgotten to take note of the spectrum of beauty found within the Black community. However, we should acknowledge, with pride and support, that supermodel Tyra Banks did make history by being the first Black woman to grace the cover of one of the major sports magazines. And as beautiful as that sister is, with looks that can stand on their own on any mainstream-magazine cover, she had to share her first cover with another model. Fortunately her mainstream selling appeal was finally recognized and appreciated, and she was granted a solo spread on a follow-up cover a year or so later.

I received this e-mail from a sister who was feeling down because she was concerned that her looks impacted negatively on her chances of having good relationships.

Dear Dr. Grace Cornish,

Is it true when it comes to men choosing women, almost all men don't prefer big girls/fat women? This is what my father always tells me. Sometimes it gives me very low self-esteem, especially being a darker-skinned black woman. I wasn't always big. But now I am. How do I get to feel better about myself, learn to like myself better—whether I'm small or big— and gain more self-esteem? Because to tell you the truth, that's something that's always been very, very hard for me to do.

Terri M.

SOME LIKE THEM TALL, SOME LIKE THEM SMALL; SOME LIKE THEM BIG, SOME LIKE THEM ALL!

Dear Sister Terri,

Don't you let anyone dictate how you feel about yourself. God made each of us in our particular package for a purpose. Your father may mean well, but do not let his opinion cause you to be sad. Beauty comes in all sorts of shapes, shades, and sizes.

And don't buy into the theory that men will bypass you because of your size and skin coloring. Girl, like you, I have beautiful dark skin and am "pleasantly plump." I have never had a shortage of male admirers because I really *like* and am very comfortable with who I am. Once you learn how to use your gifts to build your self-worth, you will meet the man that's right for you. However, if you're uncomfortable about your weight, then try to begin an exercise routine and good nutritional program—but I repeat, do not let anyone put you down. You know what? I'm going to personally monitor your progress. Please keep in touch with me, and let's get you into the right frame of mind, and then into the right relationship.

Talk with you soon,

Dr. Grace

WHEN IT COMES TO BROTHERS, WHICH ONE REIGNS? IS IT BEAUTY OR IS IT BRAINS?

Let's face facts. It's wonderful to feel beautiful. We can't ignore the fact that men and women spend huge amounts of money on diet products, at cosmetics counters, in hair salons and barbershops, and at health clubs to enhance their appearance. I am the first one to encourage you to pamper yourself and enhance *your exterior beauty.* But I have and will always place emphasis on *your interior beauty,* not the *false beauty* standard created and marketed by anyone else, no matter how popular it may be.

In a *Jet* magazine article called "Do Looks Outweigh Brains When Choosing a Mate?" I was asked how important outward appearances should be when choosing a significant other. Should what's inside your head count for more than your appearance? Or do looks outweigh brains when choosing a mate?

We can't deny that looks are important because two people have to be attracted to each other. However, we mustn't operate by a certain standard because what may look appealing to one person may not appeal to another. Fortunately contemporary Black men and women are appreciating one another's looks more. Many realize that our definition of beauty cannot and should not be the same as that of White America.

How you look may attract you to someone, but it's how you think that will stand the test of time. If you are creating a relationship on looks alone, it may last six months or even six years, but it won't last forever. Your brain is important in maintaining a lasting relationship because it will supply you with ways to keep each other enchanted, interested, and intrigued by constantly growing and learning new things together. The reason many people leave, or get bored with each other, is usually because one person stopped growing.

Men's perceptions are changing at a rapid pace today. They are forming their own opinions of beauty and are not placing false beauty standards on their list when choosing a long-term mate. One of the reasons for this new awareness is that men are becoming more spiritual. Many are more comfortable with themselves and do not rely on a trophy wife to boost their egos.

SESSION 4: REMOVING THE FALSE-BEAUTY MASK: "LEARN TO BE WITTY, BUT ACKNOWLEDGE THAT YOU'RE ALREADY PRETTY"

Sis, I wanted to explore this subject even more deeply and provide a clearer picture of what men really think. So I contacted and interviewed male advocate Carl Hendricks, who is a motivational coach and author of *Rootin' for the Crusher.*

Dr. Grace: Carl, beauty seems to be a key ingredient that attracts a man and keeps him interested in someone. What are some other qualities that men are looking for in a woman?

Carl: Integrity. Personality. Physical attractiveness is very important, but it varies according to different preferences. If a woman feels beautiful from the inside, it comes across to a man, and he finds that quite attractive. Women who are consistent in their behavior, maintain their ideals, and respect their man's viewpoint tend to attract men who are up-front and not looking to run a "game." These women can usually detect and avoid the "players" more easily than their more susceptible sisters.

Dr. Grace: Let's get real and break this down further. Many Black women have been led to believe that their features, complexion, and figures are less than ideal. This has caused confusion, pain, and sometimes even self-hatred. Most sisters are harsh critics of their looks. They compare themselves to magazine and media images, and they unavoidably feel less beautiful. They are not aware that that "look" is achieved by special makeup and lighting, then airbrushed and retouched several times in the photo lab. By comparing themselves to what is, in effect, an artificial standard, these women feel that they cannot measure up. And because they think so little of themselves, they frequently settle for men who are unhealthy matches and are less than they desire or deserve.

Carl: Women have to feel truly beautiful from the inside. It makes little sense to get too wrapped up in the latest fad because: (a) fads change and may be replaced by something else by the time you [adjust to] them, and (b) worse yet, [they] may be something you never really wanted in the first place. The best way to achieve a sense of pride and bring out your own natural attributes is by being true to what you really believe.

KEEPING IT REAL: SELF-ASSURED MISTERS PREFER SELF-CONFIDENT SISTERS

Dr. Grace: When companies advertise the false "ideal look" of the moment, they are using a selling gimmick to convince us to buy "beauty" through the particular product they are peddling. Somewhere along the line, both Black men and women have bought into the advertised mainstream ideal in varying degrees. We cannot ignore the fact that even "grass-roots" rap videos seem to be promoting their melanistic version of "the look." Carl, how does this affect men's perception of women?

Carl: What you described is a classic example of subliminal seduction, and it affects society as a whole. Advertisers use the gimmick you described—and some far more subtle and just as effective. Far too many men buy into this mass psychology involved in these ad campaigns. But some do not. Self-confident and self-assured men prefer women who are not easily swayed by false ideals. In relationships it is crucial to remember you are your own special person with divine qualities within you. And you should not get involved with any man who cannot appreciate you for who you are.

Dr. Grace: Thank you, brother—excellent point! The healthiest gift a sister can give herself and a mate is to get in touch with her inner self, enhance her exterior, and respect the entire package.

SESSION 5: REMOVING THE "MARS/VENUS" MASK: "GOTTA RESPECT EACH OTHER'S WORTH, RIGHT HERE ON PLANET EARTH"

Let me share with you a portion of what award-winning journalist Edmund Lewis, editor of the *Louisiana Weekly,* had to say about my approach to helping Black men and women create healthy relationships. In his popular editorial, "A Man's World, but . . . ," he wrote:

> I spent part of Sunday, October 18, hanging out with Dr. Grace Cornish, author of *10 Bad Choices That Ruin Black Women's Lives.* It was truly an uplifting and enlightening experience, not to mention a lot of fun.
>
> I have to admit that when I first heard about "Dr. Grace's" book, I thought, Oh Lawd, another one of those somebody-done-somebody-wrong books. But she reassured me that her book was "brother friendly." And as I listened to a radio interview the good doctor did while in New Orleans and had an opportunity to sit down and exchange ideas and theories about male-female relationships with her, I came away impressed

not only with this charismatic, compassionate sister but also with her powerful message. I was inspired.

Dr. Grace Cornish isn't one of those bitter scorned women who is seeking to blame brothers for every problem women experience in the world. While she acknowledges that some men have done some *purty* awful things to women that are inexcusable, her goal is to empower women by showing them how crucial it is that they stop, look and think before leaping into new relationships. Although she aptly runs down some of the games men run on the women in their lives, she does so only to let women know that they are not alone and need not be ashamed for making bad choices in the past. She tells them that what really matters is that they learn from the mistakes of the past to make wiser choices in the future.

I am not the least bit surprised that a large number of white women are also responding to *10 Bad Choices That Ruin Black Women's Lives* because it has a message that is universal. For example, Dr. Grace says that it is very important that no one—male or female—sits around waiting for a soulmate to come walking into his or her life. No, the "down time" represents an opportunity to fuel our spiritual and intellectual growth, and to work on becoming the kind of people we would like to marry. Without nurturing and loving ourselves, she says, none of us will be someone others would want to meet and marry. We need to use that time wisely.

Seek a soul mate, don't settle for a stalemate

The dating game is a very serious matter these days, with very serious consequences. With AIDS and other sexually transmitted diseases, rape, child molestation, suicide and domestic violence making headlines in the nation's newspapers daily, it's imperative that women *and* men choose their partners wisely. Even casual dating can have tragic results these days.

One of the theories I have about dating is that oftentimes it is difficult for men and women to hook up with their soulmates because so many people settle for Mr. Right Now, or Ms. Right Now, or the first sweet thing that comes along. While that may look, at first glance, like a choice that is personal and won't affect anyone else, what it effectively does is take men and women out of the dating pool and decrease the number of eligible bachelors and bachelorettes available to play the dating game. [In effect, you may never connect with your soul mate because you are already married to someone who really doesn't love or appreciate you, but you think you can't do better, and you merely cope with it.] It is therefore selfish, thoughtless and reckless, not to mention dishonest, to commit to a relationship with someone for whom you have no substantial feelings. And it is from these kinds of unions that people emerge bitter, angry and confused, and ready to pass on that negative energy to others.

It's truly wealthy to have a love that's healthy

Grace helped me to understand that a great deal more is at stake in relationships than most of us think. It's not just about broken hearts, bruised egos or unhappiness; without healthy, productive male-female relationships, and healthy family life, a healthy African-American community is simply not possible. These relationships are, then, the basic building blocks of Black America. Without black-on-black love, our survival and prosperity is anything but certain.

One of the things sorely lacking in today's relationships is the emphasis on courtship; the period when a man and woman really take the time to get to know one another and determine whether or not they are truly compatible. Dr. Grace's eyes danced as she described the process of a man and woman initially getting acquainted and all that that entails. Not only is a lengthy courtship practical and prudent, it can add a great deal of spice and excitement to any relationship, she said.

Although most marriages begin with a church wedding, all too often spirituality is neglected and overlooked by many of today's young couples. The Creator who brought two people together to form a union is the same Creator who will stand by these brothers and sisters through good and bad times and direct their paths daily. When couples quarrel, they should resolve their differences with the Creator in mind, and when they celebrate something, they should rejoice with the Holy Spirit. In order for any couple to have a fighting chance of making it, the Creator must be allowed to be their guide and traveling companion.

Let's drop the defense because in a deeper sense, we're both sitting on the same side of the fence

Whether we choose to admit it or not, all of us, male and female, need love, friendship and companionship. All of us need to know what it feels like to have someone who loves us for who we are, not what we are, who we know, or what we own.

Finally, inequity and unfairness in relationships is something all of us need to be concerned about because without relationships that nurture and inspire both partners, the world will continue to be as cold and unforgiving as it is today and love will continue to be seen as a battlefield where only the strong and merciless survive. The "cold war" between the sexes is a war in which there can be no winners, only losers with an ful of regrets and hearts filled with bitterness and pain.

That needs to change.

WE CAN BEST RELATE WHEN WE CAN COMMUNICATE

Yes, indeed, my dear brother Edmund, it needs to change. Now is a good time. Sis, throughout this chapter I have shared with you the true heart-to-heart feelings coming directly from the men themselves. These brothers are real. They are kind, compassionate, and caring individuals just like you and me.

If you noticed in the "removing the mask" sessions, the main point that each brother kept referring to was *communication*. Here's a terrific tip that many leading therapists use when making a breakthrough in couples therapy. It is known as the "I Instead of You" method. This is sure to sharpen your communications skills and instantly improve the way you open up to each other.

EXERCISE: The positive state to talk with a mate— "I Instead of You"

1. *Do say:* "I believe that we're so busy with work that we've not spent enough fun time together lately."

Don't say: "You're always so busy; you never spend enough time with me anymore."

2. *Do say:* "I noticed that you seem to be going through a lot and don't want to burden me, but I am here for you and will listen to anything you would like to share with me."

Don't say: "Why do you clam up instead of talking and letting me know what you're thinking and how you're feeling?"

3. *Do say:* "I'm so glad you're such a decent and honorable man. I wish more men would be as incredible and honest with their mates as you are with me."

Don't say: "You had better not cheat on me, bastard."

Sis, I hope that as a result of these sessions you now have the practical and effective tools to communicate in a manner that will help you to not only unmask and avoid any, and all, would-be tricksters, but that they will also guide you into uncovering and discovering some genuine, decent, and sincere brothers that you can bond with.

to understand one another, you gotta bond with a brother

Sis, here's a profound truth I discovered that will save you from future headaches and heartaches: One of the major reasons women have not yet found their individual Mr. Right is that most women do not have enough healthy, non-sexual friendships with men. Therefore, when a guy comes along who seems nice, they allow him into their hearts before they have gotten to know his true character. The simple but unfortunate truth is most women are not used to having kind, decent, and chivalrous male friends in their lives.

Because popular belief tells us that men and women cannot be friends, we have a tendency to not even try to have platonic relationships with members of the opposite sex. This tendency has caused much of the misunderstanding and miscommunication between the sexes. We have bought into the myth that we are from different planets, have alienated each other, and have been abused and misused by each other.

To this end, Dr. Johnetta B. Cole, former president of Spellman College, acknowledges, "Men may be from Mars and we womenfolks from Venus, but we have got to figure out how to live better with each other right here on Earth."

Amen to that! Sis, it's time to stop viewing each other as

competitors, and instead, view each other as companions. Think about this: How many really good, courteous, and genuine male friends do you have, with absolutely no strings attached? I urge you to surround yourself with at least three platonic, kind, and supportive male friends. One sister describes this as having "a pair and a spare." This way you'll be accustomed to being around men who treat you with the respect you deserve, and in turn, you will learn to expect the same treatment and characteristics from the men you become romantically involved with.

As the relationship expert for *Belle* magazine (no longer in circulation), I wrote the *Can We Talk Openly?* column, which was in a "he says/she says" format. For each issue, I interviewed a different man to create a balanced male/female view for our readers.

One particular story, "Love, Respect, and No Sex," was such a favorite among readers and was responded to with such a large amount of mail that the editor in chief asked me to follow up with a second part. The invited male guest for that month's editorial was one of my very own best platonic male friends, Lingsworth Pendley, a building contractor and an involved parent. The overall theme of the piece showed how honest, nonsexual friendships between Black men and women are very rare, yet quite necessary to help create more nurturing, understanding, and healthy love relationships within our race. I find it quite appropriate to share the flavor of our dialogue with you here.

LET'S BE OPEN AND HONEST, SIS—NO TOUCHING AND FEELING IN YOUR PLATONIC DEALING

Dr. Grace: Lingsworth, you and I have been good friends for quite a few years now. What do you have to say to people who believe men and women cannot be "just friends"?

Lingsworth: It's a myth. I don't know why we've bought into it, but a man can be friends with a woman without expecting any physical relationship to evolve, if he's smart enough to recognize that there is a lot to be given and gained without physical interactions.

Dr. Grace: What makes friendship between men and women work?

Lingsworth: The same thing that makes friendships work between any two people. They must have mutual respect for each other. They should also have common interests, things that they can do together to develop a bond. If two people can have fun without demanding anything from each other and just simply enjoy each other's conversation and company, they will become friends. It has to do with accepting the person for who [she is] and dealing with [her] on that level.

Dr. Grace: What makes a good friend?

Lingsworth: Loving someone unconditionally and being loved by that person in the same way. You will do things for that person because you love [him] and will not expect anything in return.

Dr. Grace: Do you think most men are able to be just friends with women, or is that rare?

Lingsworth: It's rare, but not impossible. A lot of men, but not all, will many times misinterpret a woman's affection and begin to believe that something more is developing. For instance, if a woman gives a man a friendly hug, as she would to one of her girlfriends, he may think that something more than friendship will follow. However, if the woman takes her time, she'll get to know the type of man she's dealing with, and she'll find out whether or not she can trust him.

FRIENDSHIP RULE 1: YOU ARE VALUABLE ENOUGH TO GET KIND TREATMENT WITHOUT HAVING TO GIVE ANY KIND OF SEX TREATMENT

Dr. Grace: Do you think that women can accept a man's kindness as strictly friendship?

Lingsworth: What I find is that many women tend to believe that there is a motive behind a man's kindness. Most women are not used to men being kind to them unless they want sex, and as a result, if the man does a small favor for a woman, she starts worrying about what he wants. I even find that some women flirt and make sexual advances toward me just because I treat them with respect.

You know, one of the things I've always admired about you is that you have never misinterpreted my kindness. You simply accepted it as if it were your birthright, and that's why we have become such good friends.

Dr. Grace: This is true [*smiles*]. I do deserve kind treatment, and I will not settle for less. But I also believe that all women deserve the same respectful treatment and must not settle for anything less. Lingsworth, what about the games men and women play with each other—how do we get beyond them?

Lingsworth: People play games because they wish they were something that they're not. When your friendship becomes genuine, you realize you don't have to be anyone other than

who you are. When you realize tha
friend, that she likes you just the way
stop. If you love yourself, then someone
and love you. Respect is the most import
any friendship.

People, in general, make it more difficu
women to become friends because they feel th   and
woman are friends, then something must be going on. This
belief is probably why the myth that men and women can't be
friends continues to be so powerful in our society. But if we,
men and women, developed friendships with each other, our
relationships with each other would improve greatly.

Dr. Grace: Oh, yes indeed. No wonder I cherish you as
such a good friend!

CAN EX-LOVERS BE FRIENDS?

Recently, I was invited to appear on a special episode of
BET's *Oh, Drama!* talk show named after my bestseller *10
Bad Choices That Ruin Black Women's Lives.* On the set with
me was Michael Baisden, former host of the TV show *Talk
or Walk,* and bestselling author of *Never Satisfied: How and
Why Men Cheat.* During the show, he and I shared many
similar views on the dynamics that affect male/female relationships.

However, when the million-dollar question "Can you be
friends with your ex?" was brought forth, Michael and I
respectfully agreed to disagree, after we discovered we were
on opposite ends of the spectrum on this matter. He strongly
believed that once the relationship is over, so should be the
friendship. And I, on the other hand, strongly believe this is
only applicable in situations where there are still traces of
romantic sparks. In those cases you are only fooling yourself

you are "strictly friends." However, in cases where both people have severed all romantic ties, have grown beyond their onetime love connection, and have matured enough to draw a clear line of demarcation between friendship and a love relationship, then certainly they can be casual and platonic friends. The *ex* can then become an abbreviation for "exit"; which means that all forms of romantic and sexual feelings have "exited" from your connection.

FRIENDSHIP RULE 2: BOUNCE THE BED-BUDDY OUT OF YOUR BONDING

There is nothing harmful in being friends if you keep things in proper perspective. And, sis, proper perspective does not mean sleeping with your so-called friends. I've seen so many women torn up with confusion because they were having intercourse with men who told them that they did not want monogamous commitments but still wanted to be "friends." Let's stop twisting and bending the definition of friendship to suit our distorted views by stretching it to include sexual escapades. Sis, it's time to bounce the bed-buddies out of your bonding and your bedroom. Believe me, I've seen too many women hurt over these unhealthy arrangements; you are doing yourself more harm than good by letting physical ties interfere with your friendships.

LET'S GO TO THE CUTTING EDGE: CAN THERE BE FRIENDSHIP EVEN AFTER A DIVORCE?

This is a hot topic among both men and women, particularly in cases of divorce or where children are concerned. Is it possible for two people who were once romantically linked to be casual companions? Once the intimate relationship has ended—no more making up, no more breaking up—can a platonic, nonsexual relationship begin?

Many wonder, *How could someone who was once my most intimate partner become a total stranger, or even worse, my bitter enemy?* With all the chaos involved in filing legal documents, dividing property, suing for custody, and keeping your emotional self intact, can you ever be close again?

The answer is yes. However, it depends on three very important factors:

1. The conditions that led to the separation
2. The emotional state of the people involved
3. Timing

As we have heard and seen, divorce is an extremely emotionally charged experience—and many times, it ends up being a nasty situation that causes extreme distress and pain for one or both parties involved. It's often difficult for divorced couples to remain friends because the end of the marriage represents a broken contract, a broken union, and a broken trust.

However, in situations where both partners have outgrown each other, are bored, or realize that they would be better off apart, differences may be settled amicably and friendship is not ruled out. Of course, in circumstances where one party is not yet ready to let go, friendship will not likely be a part of the outcome.

Let's take a look at two examples with opposite results:

EXAMPLE ONE: *THE BITTER BREAKING*
Twenty-three years ago, Sandra and Troy were married on Sandra's eighteenth birthday. Sandra gave birth to a son when

she was twenty-two. That same year, she learned Troy had been involved in a yearlong affair with a coworker. After much deliberation and bickering, Troy filed for a divorce. By the time Sandra was twenty-five, she was a divorced single mother, supporting a son on her own.

Troy makes few or no contributions to their son's upbringing or education, and Sandra is very hurt. This is quite understandable. She has moved on with her personal life, but she admits that she is still disappointed and upset, not because Troy left her, but because he abandoned his son. Had he played an active role in his son's life, Sandra said that she and Troy would have been able to maintain a casual, nonsexual friendship.

EXAMPLE TWO: *THE BETTER BONDING*

Melvin's situation differs from Sandra's. LaTonya, whom he was married to for six years, left him and took their two small children with her. Melvin admits that he "had a drinking problem and drove away a good woman." The divorce was a wake-up call for him, and he has cleaned up his act in the eight years since their split. Melvin has always supported his children financially, and after three years of sobriety, he maintains a civilized friendship with LaTonya.

When I asked about the formula that makes their friendship work, Melvin agreed when LaTonya said, "We do not cross the lines. We did the best with what we knew in our marriage, but we have grown past that stage. We have two beautiful children together who will always create a bond, but we keep things in perspective—no sex. We are both in our new marriages, but respect each other for what we have been through."

Melvin and LaTonya maintain a healthy friendship because they managed to remove both the bitterness and the bedroom out of their bonding.

FRIENDSHIP RULE 3: NO SEX WITH THE EX

There are many cases where couples gravitate back to each other sexually, or continue to share common possessions such as the keys to the house, credit cards, and checking accounts, even though they have relinquished their "official" and legal rights to do so. Ex-lovers must set boundaries after the relationship ends. Two of the most sensitive areas are sex and money. Settle your financial differences (legally if you have to), and keep your intimate activities in perspective.

Sis, let's take this to the limit here: There is a popular but unflattering statement that goes, "Why buy the cow when you can get the milk for free?" Well, let's flip the script, sis: "If he refuses the cow, then why should he get the milk for free?"

On that note, let's take a look at Chante's circumstance:

Dear Dr. Cornish,

You were so right when you said in the beginning of your book *10 Good Choices That Empower Black Women's Lives* that my life would be transformed, because it has. It has reassured me that I can do all things through Christ, who strengthens me (Philippians 4:13).

I am experiencing a little difficulty in my love life at the moment. It is very similar to the young lady at the end of chapter 2 [in *10 Good Choices*] who wanted to be friends with her lover, but felt that it wouldn't happen because they were intimate before they were friends. Well, my situation is like that in the sense that I do already love this man and I am praying that God will bless this union. We are not in a committed relationship because he says that he is not looking for anything serious at this moment. I am fine with that because I know that I have things that I need to make me whole before I am complete with someone else.

But I don't seem to believe him or trust him when he says

that he is not in a committed relationship with someone else, mainly because his best friend told me that he was. I do feel that the information I got from his best friend was information that I pried into and that it probably never would have been brought to me if I didn't initiate [getting] it, but I did; and I found out that he has a girlfriend whom he has been with for three years. When I asked him about it, or rather accused him, he denied it and said that he has been honest with me since the first day that we met.

To make things a bit more confusing, a mutual friend got married, and Kevin brought another girl with him to the wedding, which he told me about the night before, and I expressed to him that I was not going to be happy about seeing him with another woman. I asked him why didn't he ask me to attend with him, since we were dating, [and] he said that our mutual friend invited him and his date because he knew of them as a couple when they were together. He then said that they were not together and that it was a little complicated to discuss at that time.

Since then I have left lengthy messages on his voice mail expressing how I feel. Finally we talked about our situation, and he stated that he doesn't believe that he has led me on because he hasn't made any promises to me, and just because he likes me doesn't mean that he is obligated to tell me his story or his past.

I disagree. He said that he missed my calm and relaxed demeanor and that he wanted us to get back to having fun and getting to know each other. He is not looking for a long-term relationship right now, and he is not involved in one with me or anyone else. He wants us to be friends and see what happens from there.

Let's do the math:
casual friendship + uncommitted Sex = major confusion

The problem is that I already love this man and I am jealous of this other woman. It bothers me to know that when he is not with me, he may be with her. When we are together we have such a good time with each other, and sex is not always involved, but it is in the equation. I have decided that I have to take it out of the equation in order to continue our friendship and [maintain] my sanity. Do you think that I am wasting my time, and making something more [of it] than what it is? Or should I follow what my heart is telling me, which is to first be true to myself and to give this relationship a chance to grow at its own pace? I would really appreciate if you would respond back.

    Sincerely,
    Chante L.

FRIENDSHIP RULE 4: SIS, KEEP YOUR MIND OPEN AND YOUR LEGS CLOSED

My dear sister Chante,

I feel the urgency of your emotional turmoil hidden between the lines of what you've written. Since you've mentioned that this is affecting your "sanity," I am not going to take up time with reasons why you should leave this situation. You have already written them all—but I will say this: Friends do not have sex with friends. If any man tells you that, it's a cop-out. If he wants friendship, then, sis, keep your mind open and your legs closed. Do not let anyone use friendship as an excuse to sample your sexuality and brush you off as it pleases him. That's ridiculous. You deserve better than that. Do not get intimate with casual "friends."

In all honesty, I believe that deep down inside *you know what to do,* but it's extremely painful and confusing because *you don't know how to do it.* So, I'm going to help you process the pain, get it out of your system, and move beyond this unhealthy arrangement. Sis, trust me here—there are thousands of women who have been where you are now, and many are still going through it. I'm going to share with you the method that I have used in my empowerment seminars and weekend "Restoration Retreats" to help thousands of sisters in the United States and abroad to get through this.

How to cope and renew your hope

You can't skate over it or run around it; you've got to move through the pain and release it from the inside. Allow me to walk with you through your emotions.

Does this sound familiar? You've tried your best in the relationship. You knew he wasn't the best for you, but you hung in there, hoping he would treat you better, or return the feelings you had for him, but all of a sudden things changed. He changed the course of things. He decided to call a halt to the deeper connection you longed for. How do you cope? How do you hold on to your sanity? How do you keep on? How do you move on?

Day in, day out; night after night, he monopolizes your thoughts. You can't get him out of your mind. Life feels meaningless. People tell you to have patience, and the right love will come along someday. But you don't want to hear that right now; all you want is him. You start to think of all the things you could have done to keep him, to make him want you exclusively, to make it work. You think of all the good times you shared. How good he made you feel. How much you miss him. How very badly you need him right now.

You daydream about him coming back and staying in your arms, and how good it will feel. You wonder who he's with, what does she have over you, what is he doing, and if he ever thinks about you the way you always think of him. You yearn for this man; your entire system is consumed with his being.

As time passes, you begin to get tired of your own tears. You start to get upset for thinking of this man because you realize that he has designed the course of things, has dis-

tanced himself, and your tears are neither changing h
mind nor bringing him into a healthy relationship with
you. You start to fight the visions, thoughts and memories of
this estranged lover, and the enchanting times you spent
together. . . . *Don't!*

Here's a twist—it's okay to remember
the good times and the kiss

That's right—*don't* fight it. Allow yourself to remember all
the good times you shared. Enjoy your memories. *But,* be fair
to yourself and give yourself equal time to visualize the bad,
hurtful, and unhappy memories as well. Think of all the unfair
and painful things he has done to you—the things that made
you mistrust him. The things that didn't make you feel good
about yourself, that made you feel uncomfortable, unwanted,
unloved. Visualize all the unpleasantness and embarrassment
that he has put you through. Think about the personality conflicts between you. Then, sis, weigh it all up. Write your feelings down. Make a *good* list and a *bad* list of your relationship
with him. Now, answer honestly: Was this relationship fair or
healthy for you?

It may take some time to get to this point, but you should
strive to hold no hard feelings against him. Realize that he was
unable to appreciate your worth. Don't be angry or saddened
by his decision; instead, feel compassion for him. Force yourself to really wish him the best, and love him from a distance
if you have to. Next, turn the matter over to God. Know that
you did your best, but you have to move on. Know within
your very center that you deserve much better treatment than
this. You deserve healthy love, sis!

Don't think of replacing him with someone else right away.
Instead, concentrate on getting to know yourself better. How
does this make you feel about yourself? How can you nurture
yourself? What are you afraid of? Is it loneliness? If yes, why?

**When the Comforter is in the equation,
it's healing time for your heart's abrasion**

Talk it over with your intuitive inner self. There's a Comforter that we each have within us. It is a gift from God, as promised to us by our elder brother, the Divine Nazarene: "Do not let your heart be troubled, neither let it be afraid. . . . If it were not so, I would have told you so. . . . And I will pray to the Father, and He will give you another Comforter, that will abide with you forever. . . . I will not leave you comfortless; I will come to you. . . ." (John 14).

Sis, our individual Comforter is there to console us in all situations. Whether we choose to term it as the Spirit of Truth, the Holy Spirit, or the Divine Helper, it doesn't matter. The point is it's there to guide and comfort us at all times.

Be open with your Comforter. Let your Comforter know that you are afraid of being lonely, unloved, and growing older alone. Talk as you would to a best friend. Ask for warmth, inner peace, and guidance, then sleep at night (or nap in the afternoon) with the assurance that your prayers are being answered. Each time disturbing thoughts of the estranged boyfriend, or any other situations that make you afraid, surface, let your Comforter guide you.

**In time you'll discover the relief of being free
from an unhealthy-minded lover**

Just take it one day at a time. Eventually you'll genuinely feel grateful to the ex for releasing you to achieve more in life. You'll realize that it was a blessing in disguise, because what you shared was never healthy love. Because healthy love helps you to bring out your best; there is no nonsense or confusion in the "equation." This profound truth is confirmed in 1 Corinthians 13:4–6: "Love is kind and is not jealous; love does not brag and is not arrogant; does not act unbecomingly; it does not seek its own; does not rejoice in unrighteousness."

Sis, to sum it up, healthy love does not lie, does not hurt, does not sleep with you and call it friendship, does not threaten your sanity; instead, it makes you feel really good about yourself. I strongly suggest that you take a long vacation from this distorted "friendship," and take the time to mend the wear and tear on your emotions so that you can attract the good and healthy relationship that you really and truly deserve, my sister. Once you've repaired your emotions and put things in proper perspective, then you can work on building a casual, nonsexual, and constructive friendship with him if you choose. May God bless you through the process. I really care, and want you to do well. Please keep in touch from time to time, and let me know how you're doing.

With love,
Dr. Grace

FRIENDSHIP RULE 5: IF YOU'RE NOT MEANT TO BE LOVERS, THAT DOESN'T MEAN YOU CAN'T BE GREAT FRIENDS

Leaving a relationship is hardly ever going to be pleasant. But it is possible to build a friendship after we have passed through the unpleasantness of letting go. Many people are mismatched in unhealthy intimate relationships. Keep in mind that just because you are not meant to be together as lovers does not mean you can't be great platonic friends.

There is an old, wise saying that goes, "Whatever is truly yours can never be taken away from you." Sis, repeat this until it soaks into the very center of your system: "Whatever is truly yours can never be taken away from you." You'll understand, embrace, and enjoy the fullness of this universal truth when you finally experience the healthy love you deserve.

Your ex, whether an ex-husband, ex-lover, ex-boyfriend, or ex-bed-buddy, was not your true soul mate. That's why you are not together today. Sis, on the higher spiritual scheme of things, you could very well be going through a cleansing-and-preparing process at the moment. God is a God of order, and we've got to get rid of the old to make room for the new. Biblical wisdom tells us, "Do not put new wine into old bottles; otherwise the bottles burst, and the wine pours out and the bottles are ruined; but put new wine into new bottles, and both are preserved."

That's my purpose throughout this book, sis, to restore and recondition you to become a "new bottle," so that you may fill your life with "new wine" (healthy love). We cannot move from one stage to another without proper cleansing. If we do not empty out the hurtful memories and ill feelings toward men, we will continue to weigh ourselves down with over-stuffed emotional baggage. It's time to take the duct tape off the dilapidated luggage and get a brand-new set of traveling suitcases so that we may enjoy a lighter and more pleasant journey. This is not in any way meant to nullify some of the horrendous, horrific, and cruel deeds that have been done in the past, but in all fairness, how can anyone blame the entire male gender for the acts done by a fraction of the population? That would be both defeating and damaging. Healthy love cannot survive under these conditions. To preserve it, we have to preserve ourselves.

FRIENDSHIP RULE 6: "A FEW BAD APPLES DON'T SPOIL THE ENTIRE ORCHARD"

Self-preservation means releasing the anger and antagonism that may be keeping us anchored at a base level in life. It's not about the people who have caused you grief or great pain—do not give them that power to dictate your emotions any longer—it's about your releasing the energy that is holding you captive within your own body temple. Walk with me through this, sis. I wouldn't advise you to do something that I would not do myself. I had to learn to forgive, and empty out, so that I could move forward on life's path—and move to the next level and attract a higher form of love. And I did both! This is real—it's not about who can outplay whom. It's about building healthy friendships with our counterparts so that we can dissolve the facade and the negative vibrations that have us repelling each other's friendship and keep us running in opposite directions.

I strongly believe that when a door closes on an unhealthy relationship, and you have empowered your life, God will always open up a healthy one for you, but sometimes we just have to spend a little time in the hallway. Sis, when we are in life's hallway, it is a chance to build healthy friendships and prepare ourselves to walk through greater doorways.

WHEN ONE DOOR CLOSES, GOD ALWAYS OPENS ANOTHER, BUT SOMETIMES WE HAVE TO SPEND A LITTLE TIME IN THE HALLWAY

It does not matter how many wrong doors you have walked through in the past, or how many revolving doors have spun you around in whirlwind relationships. What really matters is what you do with your time in the hallway, today, right now, while waiting for the right door to open. If you believe this with all your heart, it will happen. I am living proof of this reality—I have stepped through a few wrong doors myself, but thank God, years ago, I decided to stand in His hallway until I got myself restored and conditioned for a higher form of love. Healthy love is available to each and every one of us.

In Revelation 3:20, God says, "Behold, I stand at the door and knock; if anyone hears my voice and opens the door, I will come in to her and will dine with her, and she with me." Sis, use your time wisely while waiting in the hallway.

FRIENDSHIP RULE 7: HAVING GOOD FEMALE/MALE COMPANIONSHIPS CAN HELP YOU MOVE FROM UNHEALTHY RELATIONSHIPS

The following letter is from a sister who is currently standing in God's hallway, waiting patiently, yet joyously, for her door to open so that she can step over the threshold to a higher form of living and loving. She was able to close the unhealthy door behind her with the friendship of a compassionate and sensitive man who helped her to look at herself "through new eyes." Through her story you'll see how forming good friendships with supportive men can help you to not only avoid but also to get out of unhealthy unions.

Dear Dr. Cornish,

In 1993 I married my baby's father. Before our one-year anniversary, he had cheated on me with another woman who also had a child for him in 1994—two weeks before I had my daughter. Instead of leaving this man, I stayed with him for four more years, enduring constant mental and emotional abuse.

I knew I deserved better, but I felt that no one else would want me. I neglected my children and myself, trying to make this man love me, but how could he love me when I didn't love myself?

In 1998 I practically bottomed out, and things became too much for me to bear. I was evicted from my home while my children spent the summer with my father. I was forced to move in with my mother-in-law. At this time, my husband and I weren't together, but that was where he was every weekend (his mother's house!). I had started the summer semester at a local community college because I was determined to make a better life for myself and my children. Unfortunately, I still loved this man and wanted him in my life. So I tried everything that I could, but still no dice.

By the time my son started kindergarten that year, I was situated enough to have a three-bedroom apartment in the projects. Social Service paid for my daughter's day care while I went to school full-time. I made a decision to leave my husband alone and get on with improving my life and the lives of my children. I asked God to forgive me for my neglect and treatment of them over the past five years.

My husband came back, and even though I knew it was doing more harm than good, I let him stay with me on the weekends. By this time I had found out that he had had a second child by the woman he was seeing when we first got married. And he was also living with a White woman from his job in another city during the week.

A brother-friend in need is a brother-friend indeed

Somewhere around the winter of 1999, I met a man through a mutual friend. We talked on the phone every night. There was nothing romantic about it. It was just two people in need of someone to talk to. The more I spoke with this man, the more I realized I had to get out of this hell that I had let myself into. He never encouraged me to leave my husband. He never gave an opinion on it one way or the other. He made me look at myself through new eyes.

I saw how I had picked myself up and instead of letting this situation destroy me and my family, I had taken steps to improve my life. The last step I needed to take was to finally cut Terrance loose and get him out of my life for good, because until I did that, any changes I made would be useless and a waste of time.

Two days later, [a] hurricane swept through—I told Terrance I wanted my house key back and I wanted a divorce. Seven months later, I moved back to my hometown, transferred to another community college, and continued my education. I graduated this past May with my degree in computer science and systems technology. I still see my soon-to-be ex-husband when he comes and gets the kids. And as hard as it is, I bear no grudges toward him or his women. That takes too much energy that I can't afford to waste.

Your books have helped immensely with my healing process, and I want to thank you very much for being one of the few people that understand. I still have a long way to go, but it helps to know that I am definitely not alone.

You wouldn't believe the difference in my life so far. My children and I started reciting this affirmation every morning:

I am Black! (Capital *B!*)
I am Beautiful!
I am Smart!
I am of God!
Therefore, I am Somebody!

Thank you again, Dr. Cornish, for making my healing process a whole lot easier.
Donna A.

You're very welcome, my dear. You are no doubt on an empowering and healthy path. I am so proud of you.

What a positive example this sister is for turning one's life around. Isn't it amazing how healthy dialogue with the opposite sex can help you to appreciate your value and self-worth through new eyes?

EXERCISE: Exploring my feelings: Can I be fond of a brother-sister bond?

1. Do I believe the myth that men and women can't be friends? Why, or why not?

2. Does it seem strange or uncomfortable to picture myself in a nonsexual friendship with a pleasant man? Why, or why not?

3. Do I currently have any really good male friends? *Brian Smalls* *Ivan*

4. Is it possible for me to begin to sustain a healthy and supportive sister-to-brother bond?

5. Do I have one or a few brothers in mind with whom I would like to establish a closer friendship?

6. Am I willing to be a sister-friend to have a brother-friend?

7. What are my greatest fears about bonding with a brother-friend?

8. How would I feel about asking a man's advice about another man?

9. If I had a good brother-friend as close as a best sister-friend, would I abandon him if people didn't understand our friendship? Why, or why not?

I would love to know your answers to these questions, especially to the last one. The following is a case in which a sister has to make a very difficult decision whether or not to give up her best male friend and confidant because her husband doesn't believe that men and women should be friends. Generally speaking, the first instinct would probably be to advise her to loosen the ties a bit if it's interfering with her marriage. However, when you read her story, you'll see that it's because of this healthy brother-friendship that she has been able to endure this unhealthy marriage for so long.

Dear Dr. Cornish,

I'm a married woman, and the mother of one child whom I love very much. I have been married seventeen years to the same man. We have had our ups and downs. He is a drinker, and sometimes he is very hateful toward me as a person. I know that you said in your books [that] you have to leave [when you are being abused and/or beaten], but sometimes I'm afraid of being alone even though I know that God is with me.

We have a rocky marriage because of [his] drinking and him not wanting to see my friends and family. He said they'll turn me against him. I told him that the only one who can turn me against him is him. My love for him is not there, but I respect the good job he has done in helping to raise our daughter. But, I also told our child that men are not like her dad. There are good men that don't call you names and undermine your way of life and feelings.

My husband is a good person, but he lives in the past. He can't seem to let go of what his father did to him and how his first wife treated him. I told him I can't change the past; all you can do is make a good future for yourself. He still fights, and his drinking makes it worse.

I have had a friend for twenty-six years. We have a close relationship and have never slept together, even though people have said otherwise. He was there for me when my father died. He was there for me when my nephew took his life which [turned] all our lives upside down (but we are working through it slowly). When I needed someone to talk to without being judged, he [has] been there.

He has been good to me, and we share our ups and downs. We laugh at our children and life. And we made it through all that has happened to both of us. [However] I need to make a choice. My husband doesn't want me to talk to or see my friend because he said men and women can't be friends. But it is very hard to say good-bye because of our closeness. As for me, I know my heart and my sense of being will miss him very much. I gave him up once before to please everyone in my life. One day he came back, and it's been a good friendship. He helps me [to] know I can do anything I put my mind to do when my husband says I can't do it.

You have shown me another way of helping myself go on, even when they are trying to pull me down. Thank you, Dr. Cornish.

Thank you,
Lydia D.

FRIENDSHIP RULE 8: IT'S A BLESSING TO HAVE A GOOD FRIEND ON HAND, WHETHER IT'S A WOMAN OR WHETHER IT'S A MAN

Dear Sister Lydia,

This is a difficult one to answer, but I'll do my best. It's difficult because on the one hand, you have a husband of seventeen years who is trying to control you by demanding that you isolate yourself from your family and friends. (Big mistake!) And his being an alcoholic makes his behavior even more irrational. Now, on the other hand, you have a caring, nonsexual relationship of twenty-six years with a male friend who has helped you through many rough times in life. Presently you are faced with the dilemma of having to choose one or the other because your husband, and others, do not understand the nature of your friendship.

Honestly, in my opinion, your husband does not have the right to demand that you give up your friend, unless you can also demand that he give up his friend (the bottle) in return. And that still doesn't make it right. You said he is a good man, yet unfortunately he has been disappointed throughout his lifetime, and in turn, he has turned to alcohol as an escape. I suggest that instead of severing all ties with your good friend, explain to him the pressure you are facing and ask him to understand while you try to coax your husband into a Twelve-Step Program to sober up and restore his self-worth, so that he will stop taking out his frustration on you.

Sis, I know it's not an easy decision to make, and whatever you decide to do, ask yourself which situation gives you peace of mind. What makes Lydia happy? You know one of the worst things on this journey called life is to have someone constantly belittle you and tell you that you can't accomplish much, as your husband does. And one of the most joyous things is to be blessed with a good friend, be it a guy-friend or a girlfriend, who constantly coaches you on and looks out for your best interests, as your friend does.

Sis, only you can decide which is more important to Lydia at this moment. Take your time, think about it deeply, and choose wisely. If you decide that you would like to create and maintain a healthy balance by keeping both your marriage and your friendship, then that can work if your husband seeks some sort of counseling. In the meantime, you can take it to the highest Counselor of all—God. Keep praying, sis, and I'll keep praying for you also. I've placed your letter on my personal Bible. God always works in mysterious ways. Please write to me and let me know what you have decided to do.

> With sincere regards,
> Dr. Grace

I'm sure you'll agree with me that Lydia has a very important decision to make. You know, it's a pity that she is placed in a predicament where she has to choose between a healthy friendship and an unhealthy relationship. Which would you choose, sis? That's a difficult decision, isn't it?

Well, wouldn't it be best if you could have both in one man—a healthy friendship and a healthy relationship completely intertwined in one package? You will get it. I did it, and so will you. Trust me, by the time you have completed all the steps in this book, you will not settle for less.

FRIENDSHIP RULE 9: NOT EVERY WOMAN'S FRIEND SHOULD BE HER MATE, BUT EVERY WOMAN'S MATE SHOULD BE HER FRIEND

I am frequently interviewed and featured in *Jet* magazine for the "Lifestyles" section, which deals with all sorts of relationship issues. One topic that provoked an extremely large influx of mail was "Will Love Last Longer If You Are Friends First?" This generated a lot of interest because many people didn't realize the importance of friendship in their relationship. For example, a lot of couples claimed they loved each other, but they really didn't *like* each other. They didn't like each other's personalities, habits, or characteristics. Therefore, they didn't enjoy going places and doing things together. And because of this, the brilliant light that once surrounded their love life had become quite dim and dull. Their lives had become routine, so they welcomed my advice on building and keeping friendship in a relationship.

This is important because as friends first, you like and respect each other above everything. You are not looking to control or belittle each other. You are equally grounded, kind, and honest, and are genuinely interested in each other's happiness. Without true friendship, some people are on their best behavior until they cross the threshold. Once they let their guard down their true nature surfaces, and so does emotional and legal separation. With true companionship, you don't have to pretend to be someone you're not so that you can get married. Love will last longer when it comes to marriage, because your marriage and initial bonding will take place long before the wedding.

TRUE FRIENDSHIP AT ITS BEST WILL
WITHSTAND ANY LIFETIME TEST

I received this letter from a woman whose marriage of a quarter century has survived the test of time because of the kinship she feels toward her "not-too-easy-to-get-along-with" husband. Her marriage has gone through some trying times, but she is determined to bring out the best in her mate, and help him to discover his best along the way. Thank goodness for true friendship.

Dear Dr. Cornish,

I read your book *10 Good Choices That Empower Black Women's Lives.* This book inspired me to take a look at my life and make the necessary changes to make it more rewarding.

First, let me tell you about myself. I am a forty-eight-year-old wife, mother, and grandmother. I have been married for twenty-five years. I don't feel satisfied in my marriage because my husband takes me for granted and is stuck in the past. We have gone to counselors, and even though I have seen improvements in our relationship, he constantly complains that nothing has changed. Before we were married, he caught his girlfriend making out with another guy. His father cheated on his mother, and my husband has confronted his dad about it because it bothered him so. I mentioned this to our counselor, and he said that these things don't affect men and that they just brush it off. I suspect that this counselor was just trying to stay in good graces with my husband, because I know this [the cheating] weighed heavily on my husband's mind.

I don't have reason to believe my husband is cheating on me, and that is the last thing that I would do. When I am mad at my husband, I have no desire to run to the next man. Sex is not even on my mind. My decision for my marriage is to stay positive and motivate my husband to become more positive. I have faith and know that anything is possible. I've prayed for God to show me the way, so I will meditate and wait for an answer. My husband is a good man; he has heard a lot of negative things said to him in his life. He is struggling with faith because he doesn't believe that peace, joy, and happiness are his by just believing. He feels that it takes a lot of work and that it is hard to achieve. He is looking for happiness on the outside, not on the inside of himself. He says that I, the kids, and his life should make him happy.

Thanks for listening. It feels good to get this off my chest.

Sincerely,

Allison D.

FRIENDSHIP RULE 10: FRIENDSHIP IS A POWERFUL ADHESIVE THAT BONDS, AND PREVENTS BROKEN UNIONS

Dear Allison D.,

It is so wonderful to hear how positive you are in spite of all you've been through in your marriage. I have a lot of respect for you. With so many couples running to the divorce courts as soon as differences arise, I commend you for taking your marriage vows seriously. (I usually advise people to leave when there is abuse and physical danger involved.) But in your case, I think your husband has been acting like a miserable fuddy-duddy who likes to have his own way, and who can be very difficult to live with. However, with all that you've described, I can sense the kindness you feel toward your husband, who seems to love you very much but does not know how to show it. You're correct in evaluating that his behavior is a result of his past experiences.

You seem to know your husband very well, and I hope you

will pardon me for being blunt, but I think that counselor is an idiot. How dare he tell you such rubbish that men "are not affected by cheating" and they "just brush it off" and move on. Foolish advice like that will do your marriage more harm than good.

I am happy to hear that *10 Good Choices That Empower Black Women's Lives* had such a positive and helpful impact on your life. Here are three additional titles that I believe will help you, your husband, and your marriage:

1. *The Seven Principles for Making Marriage Work,* by John M. Gottman, Ph.D. (Crown)

2. *Relationship Rescue: A Seven-Step Strategy for Reconnecting with Your Partner,* by Phillip C. McGraw, Ph.D. (Hyperion)

3. *Be Loved for Who You Really Are,* by Judith Sherven, Ph.D., and James Sniechowski, Ph.D. (St. Martin's Press)

Thank you for sharing your honesty. It is very obvious that you care about your husband's best interests. Regardless of how it seems on the surface, that's a deep friendship you share—how rare and how beautiful. Just keep praying for a breakthrough, because when "the praying goes up, the blessing comes down." May God bless your marriage, and turn things around so that you can enjoy at least twenty-five more years—but twenty-five more years of healthy love, of course!

Respectfully yours,
Dr. Grace Cornish

FRIENDSHIP DOESN'T DISCOURAGE; INSTEAD, IT ENCOURAGES UNDERSTANDING

Sis, as you can see from Allison's case, a good friendship can help to keep even a challenging marriage together. If it were not for the compassion Allison felt, this marriage probably would have hit the divorce courts a decade or so ago. I truly believe that if and when Allison and her husband get the proper help, they will share a much more pleasant and healthier marriage. Allison deserves a fulfilling, healthy, and happy marriage. So do you. Can you imagine how awesome this twenty-five-year marriage would be if Allison's husband became as caring and supportive a friend to her as she is to him?

Sis, when choosing your mate, make sure he not only loves you, but he also *likes you* just for who you are. Make sure he is as much your friend as you are his, and always keep Friendship Rule 9 in mind: Not every woman's friend should be her mate, but every woman's mate should be her friend.

refusing the wrong
date and choosing
the right mate

*S*is, *the eligible Black male–shortage myth is a lie.*
All too often throughout our lives, we've been conditioned
and coached: "Girl, don't end up with a nobody. Marry a
somebody. Get yourself a nice Black doctor or lawyer who
will take care of you." Well, let's put all the cards on the table
here. Most Black men are not lawyers and doctors, and even
if they were, their professions do not guarantee that they
would treat you any better than would barbers or teachers.

It's because of early conditioning that many of us have
developed self-limiting preconceived notions of what type of
brother we should date, and what type we should sidestep.
This has contributed to the false belief that there just aren't
any "good brothers" left.

There are decent, attractive, and available brothers across
our nation—brothers who come in all shades, shapes, sizes,
and status. Contrary to popular belief, there is a wide pool of
bachelor brothers to pick, choose, and refuse if you're willing
to get out and expand your horizons. Whether your soul-mate
brother is a banker, baker, or candlestick maker, you won't be
able to recognize him if your mind is clouded with preconceived notions.

FORGET ANY FALSE RULE; DIVE REALLY
DEEP INTO THE DATING POOL

It sometimes gets too overcrowded at the safe end of the pool. For example, are you limiting your choices by believing that the man has to be taller, lighter, darker, richer, smarter, or older than you? Are you limiting your choices to a certain type? It's okay to have a preference—everyone does—but to be limited to only one certain type is self-defeating. Sis, don't just swim in the shallow end of the pool. Sometimes when you swim in shallow waters, all you end up with are shallow-minded mates.

The truth is most people, especially sisters, are afraid of plunging into deeper waters and exploring a wider range of possibilities. If this is your personal situation, then the dating pool may be drying up real fast. If you are afraid of deep-sea diving, put on a life vest of dating guidelines to keep you afloat, get into a sister-friend or brother-friend support group, but take the plunge and create new and exciting possibilities. Be open to the idea that your soul mate may be packaged in a body temple that is outside the scope of what you think is your "type."

SO WHERE DOES A SISTER BEGIN? IT'S TIME
TO EXPLORE LIKE NEVER BEFORE

Dear Dr. Grace,

I'm reading your book *10 Bad Choices,* and I am really loving it. I am a single black female, twenty-five years old, without children. I work full-time and I am in school, working on my degree in investment banking. I live alone, but I'm not lonely. Financially, I'm not where I want to be yet, but I will get there. I am having a hard time finding a mate. Because of my faith and beliefs, I would prefer someone with the same as mine. That makes it more difficult, but I'm not willing to sway in that choice.

On Friday and Saturday nights, I am home painting, writing, practicing on the piano, reading, or hanging out with family/friends, which are hobbies of mine. I am very content with myself. I don't have issues about being materialistic, insecure, or shallow. My friends always tell me that they don't understand why I am single. One friend even said, "Dionne, you are a beautiful woman on the outside, but one hell of a woman on the inside. The man that gets you will be incredibly lucky."

When I did meet someone, he just couldn't believe I was available. He even stated after dating for a while that he didn't know how he got me, that I could do better than him. I assured him that I was interested in him as a person and that [was] why I [was] with him. Then, for some reason, the relationship didn't work out because of his insecurities and infidelity; cheating on me with a woman of low morals and character.

I've moved on, and I'm ready to get back in the dating scene again. I just don't know where to begin or how to go about meeting someone. The last guy was a setup from a former friend. I really don't like the club scene. I am not interested in men at my particular church. I am not very picky; I just want a man who is emotionally secure, intelligent, and caring. I don't think that's too much to ask, but it seems to me that it's too hard to get. Do you have any advice?

Dionne

Yes, sis, you have marvelous qualities. But you have got to get out more. The man you referred to was truly an unhealthy choice. Thank goodness he's out of the picture. Whenever a man says, "Why are you with me? You deserve much better," believe him, thank him for the advice, and retreat from the relationship. He is the best judge of his own limitations and unhealthy outlook. And, no, it is not too much to want "a secure, intelligent, and caring" companion. You deserve healthy love, sis. Now, let's get started on the right dating path.

INQUIRING SISTERS WANT TO KNOW:
WHERE ARE THE BROTHERS?

First, let's explore and decipher where you're most likely to meet an appropriate mate for you. On page 74 of *10 Bad Choices,* I listed "The Top Ten Places to Meet Mr. Right," based on a national survey I conducted of 240 happily married couples and newlyweds. Here are the results that were originally published in *10 Bad Choices:*

1. Work
2. Homes and parties of mutual friends
3. Special-interest classes
4. Conferences and conventions
5. Concerts
6. Social and community events and activities
7. Church
8. Public transportation—train stations, bus stops, airport terminals
9. Libraries and bookstores
10. Weddings

Let me emphasize that this list is by no means complete. As a matter of fact, you can meet your ideal mate just about anywhere, especially when you're operating on a higher spiritual level—as in my case, where my husband, Richard, literally walked up to my front door. (You'll hear more about this story in "step 6: "Connecting with Respect has the Best Effect.")

However, I believe that this list is significant because it has worked for hundreds of couples, both before and after *10 Bad Choices* was published. I have to admit that at the onset of my research, I was a bit surprised that the number-one place couples recorded for finding their healthy love match was at the workplace. However, since the original publication of the survey, I have received numerous letters commenting on and inquiring about relationships at work, and have also been interviewed by many publications and TV shows, including *Jet* magazine and *Good Day New York,* to talk about the "pros and cons of workplace romance."

Since the large influx of women into the workforce in the 1970s, the coworker relationship has become an ongoing and very controversial subject. National studies have reflected that as many as 80 percent of working Americans have experienced some form of relationship or social-sexual encounter with a fellow employee. In an Internet survey conducted by VaultResults.com, it is reported that 59 percent of the participants confirmed that they have had an office relationship at one time or another.

Based on these astonishingly high percentages, can dating in the workplace be a good or bad choice for you? Many argue that it destroys the work relationship, while others believe it enhances their daily activities; still others are unsure. Let's look at the different experiences of two sisters.

SELMA'S STORY

Selma and Aaron were both attorneys employed by the same firm. They worked together on gathering information for a high-profile case that lasted close to three years. Halfway through this time period, they became close and eventually developed a romantic relationship. As the case intensified,

Stacey, a fellow attorney at their firm, was brought in as backup to solidify their working team. Stacey was assigned to report directly to Aaron. They, in turn, had to spend a lot of time together, and pretty soon, Selma became irate at the new working arrangement. She believed that Aaron would eventually initiate a relationship with Stacey in the same manner he had with her. Selma's jealousy started to affect her work. She was not able to concentrate on her task at hand.

Instead of gathering her share of evidence needed to win their assigned case, she was oftentimes distracted by the amount of time Aaron and Stacey spent together. This continued until one afternoon, her temper erupted in front of other employees at the firm. Selma voiced her concerns to Aaron. He very casually told her she was overreacting, and warned her not to air her personal feelings on company time. "On company time?" she exploded. "You weren't concerned with that when you were trying to screw me! Is Stacey your new flavor of the month?"

Needless to say, Selma was taken off the case. This particular workplace romance was obviously a bad choice.

KENDRA'S STORY

When Kendra first glimpsed Peter as he dashed by her desk to make the 9:00 A.M. meeting, she leaned over to her coworker Nancy and whispered, "Who is that hunk?"

"Isn't he gorgeous?" remarked Nancy. "He's the new accountant in the finance department." Kendra, who had been single for the past eighteen months, smiled at the thought of having the handsome newcomer in the department right next to hers. But she quickly dismissed her wandering thoughts as she glanced at the pile of paperwork on her desk.

She had recently experienced a bad relationship, and work

had become a safety net for her. The more occupied she was with her work, the less time she had to reminisce and brood over the past. She had become accustomed to pulling a ten- to twelve-hour shift each day. Eventually, she did repair her broken heart, but had not thought of being involved with anyone in the last year and a half.

She and Nancy always joked about their nonexistent dating life and claimed that they were "married to their work." Over the next few months, Peter became a lighthearted and harmless fantasy date in Kendra's mind. She found him attractive, thought about him often, and smiled each time he passed her desk.

As fate would have it, one afternoon they both reached the elevator doors at the same time as they were leaving the building for lunch. As they waited for the lift to stop on their floor, Peter turned to Kendra, smiled, and initiated a pleasant conversation. He told her he appreciated and looked forward to the warm smiles she flashed him daily. She blushed and asked how he was fitting into his new position at work.

Although Peter had always lived by the motto "Never mix business with pleasure," by the time the elevator arrived, he had already asked if Kendra would like to join him for lunch at the Italian deli on the corner. She accepted.

They enjoyed each other's company so much during their lunch hour that he asked her to join him again the following day, and the following, and the following. Pretty soon, their lunch date became an afternoon ritual. They found out that they had much in common, and wanted to see more of each other. They started dating outside of the workplace, and then decided to have a monogamous relationship with each other.

After ten months of dating exclusively, Peter popped the question, Kendra accepted, and they were married a year following their engagement. They have been happily married for three years. Had they believed that it was "taboo" to date on the job, they never would have found each other.

WEIGH UP YOUR OPTIONS: WHEN IT'S GOOD, IT'S TREMENDOUS, BUT WHEN IT'S BAD, IT'S HORRENDOUS

After analyzing both stories, we are brought back to the main question: Is a workplace relationship a good or bad choice? The answer is that it certainly can be a good possibility, but it really depends on both individuals involved. Sis, be aware that there are risks involved, such as employee gossip, sexual-harassment claims, and coworker tension.

However, if both people are emotionally mature enough not to vent or display their feelings in view of everyone else, it could be a most rewarding meeting ground. When it's good, it's great, but I must add, when it's bad, it's even worse. The choice is yours. But, whatever you decide, sis, just do it with respect: Respect for yourself, respect for your mate, and respect for your workplace. Respect is a key to creating healthy love. When you add in communication and discretion, you may very well have a winning formula for making any relationship work.

THE PROS AND CONS OF WORKPLACE ROMANCE

Workplace relationships can flourish if both people can come to an agreement that they are going to look out for each other's best interests and keep negative emotions out of their place of business. Couples can prevent love from going sour by agreeing that they will not do anything to harm each other's reputation and position.

What causes problems to arise in workplace romance is when two people work too closely together and either end up

their work or bringing jealousy into the office set-
can interfere with their concentration and work
productivity. There is also a chance that they may end up
competing for the same position.

The optimistic note in this seemingly pessimistic melody is
that many office romances last. I have surveyed a number of
happily married couples who met at work. One of the major
rewards of dating someone in the workplace is you already
have some background information about him, and it's easier
to get a reference. This is good news because dating can sometimes be scary nowadays and with a work and social reference
you have a better chance of selecting wisely.

In *10 Bad Choices* I provided sisters with the following
"Ten Points to Check Out Before You Let Him In." We must
first find out more about the man's behavioral pattern before
embracing him wholeheartedly. Most Black men are decent,
but there are quite a few brothers with hidden agendas whom
you would be much better off avoiding. For your own protection, make sure you know the following about anyone
before you get very intimate with him:

1. What is his full birth name?
2. What is his date and place of birth?
3. Where (and with whom) does he live?
4. Where does he work?
5. Where did he go to school?
6. Where do his parents and family live?
7. Has he ever been married before? If yes, is he legally
   divorced? For how long, and why?
8. Has he ever been arrested or had any legal troubles? If
   yes, what for, and why?
9. What are his beliefs about violence and infidelity?
10. What are his humanitarian or spiritual beliefs?

REMEMBER THESE FOUR WHEN YOU'RE READY TO EXPLORE

In an *Essence* article entitled "Is Your Man Out There?" I advised sisters on four specific points to keep in mind when exploring the dating arena:

1. **Do not be misled that all good guys are "already taken or dead."** If women would venture beyond the color of a man's collar and skin, they would have a much wider selection.

2. **Walk in stride; don't run and slide.** Avoid sprinting into a romantic and intimate relationship. Pace yourself properly by testing how it suits you. Just like a good pair of shoes, don't force the fit; instead take your time to break it in for maximum comfort and joy.

3. **Choose respect above the promise of love.** Respect is the most important aspect of any relationship. Many dates give lip service with the promise of "I love you" to manipulate you into bed. Are their actions speaking the same language as their words? Mutual respect is the vital water that quenches the thirst of compatible love.

4. **More than the billfold, go for the real gold.** Genuine worth is found in a man's heart, not in his wallet. The smooth operators, players, and big-money brothers usually come with a string of women on their coattails. These brothers often take women for granted. You are too valuable to be a groupie or become a part of anyone's harem. Go for the man who cares enough about you to cherish you, to talk with you, to listen to you, and to sit by your side when you're laid up in bed with the flu.

HOW TO RELATE ON THE DATE

Now, let's shift our discussion to some important dating dos and don'ts. The two following lists can help to get you from the dating stage to the mating stage, or to disregard unhealthy unions from the onset. Generally speaking, after the third date a pattern begins to unfold, so make sure you set the right tone from the get-go.

Global Warning: Dating Don'ts
The Seven Things You Should Never Do
During the First Three Dates

1. **Do not act overly interested in how much money he makes,** or what car, home, or assets he owns. (Believe it or not, this is a major turnoff for most men. Yes, I know, your curiosity is bubbling over, but you don't want to be misinterpreted as being more interested in his possessions than his personality.)

2. **Do not wear your heart on the outside of your blouse.** Even if you have a magical first date, do not assume you are a couple. Don't make him feel that if by the second or third date he doesn't ask you to marry him, he had better get to steppin'.

3. **Do not babble.** Men claim we women have a tendency to ramble on and on about any topic. Be friendly and lively, but not goofy. Remember to stop, listen, and encourage him to talk about himself also. This is the time period when you need to collect as much info as possible so that you can decide whether or not he's suitable for you.

4. **Do not display an attitude.** Don't act as if you're suspicious of his every word or move, or else he'll wonder why you are out with him in the first place. (Sure, you're checking him out the same way he's checking you out, but do it in a subtle and nonabrasive manner.)

5. **Do not talk about an ex-boyfriend,** ex-husband, or "some guy" you used to date. Men are highly competitive and

don't want to have some other guy tagging along on the date with them (especially if they are paying).

6. **Do not ask for money.** Many men are turned off when women ask for money, either as a loan, a gift, or to get their hair done, by the second or third date. (Yes, a lot of brothers say that quite a few women have developed this habit.)

7. **Do not lock him into a "couple's situation."** In other words, don't try to press him into going to a wedding, a family gathering, a double date, or couples' type of party. He may want to spend more time getting to know you before deciding to become an official couple. (By the way, sis, I have to insert this here—absolutely no sex in this dating period! The same way he needs time to decide if you're ideal to couple with, give yourself time to find out if he's ideal to get intimate with. Remember, for your own well-being, you should know where you're heading before you get to the bedding!)

Important Memo: Dating Dos
The Seven Things You Should Ask During the First Three Dates

1. Is he single and available?

2. What is his home number? (Don't accept a substitute of his cell, work, or beeper number.)

3. What is his home address? (No P.O. boxes, please. If a roommate is involved, make sure it's not a "bedroom mate.")

4. What are his beliefs about monogamy and infidelity?

5. Is he currently working? Does he enjoy his profession, or would he like to change it in the future?

6. What are his beliefs about violence and anger?

7. What are his spiritual beliefs?

Sis, don't be afraid to ask these questions up front. Your goal here is to find out if he's appropriate and available. If you're serious about attracting healthy love and your very own soul mate, then you cannot afford to waste your valuable time with a man who is not available. Don't even rationalize that you may eventually "win him over." Trust me on this, sis! Stop dating him immediately and save yourself from the heartache of being burned by a part-time lover man. Bid him good riddance and keep on stepping. Pay attention to the following:

Severe Warning: If He's Already Hitched, He Must Be Ditched!

The Seven Signs That Determine If He's Unavailable

1. *He has another,* but says he's planning to leave soon.

2. *He has another,* but he is not in love with her anymore.

3. *He has another,* but he is waiting until the divorce is final.

4. *He has another,* but he is only staying for the children's sake.

5. *He has another,* but they have an open relationship.

6. *He has another,* but their sex life is boring or nonexistent.

7. *He just left another,* but may be reconciling soon.

IF HE HAS ANOTHER, THEN AVOID THE BROTHER!

See the pattern, sis? There is already *another* fixture in the picture. Don't set yourself up to be played. At this stage in your life, *we* have to make sure that you avoid bad choices at all cost. Yes, *we.* You're not alone. I may not be able to be there with you in the flesh, but I'm with you in spirit and coaching you from these pages. I want to make sure you link up with a really good guy, who will be both good for you and good to you. Enough is enough! You've been through too much negative drama already. It's time for some positive rewards, sis.

In an *Essence* magazine article, "Are You Being Played?," I was asked to give some expert advice on how women could avoid being among the statistics found in the player's handbook. A few well-seasoned players were more than happy to defend their game by insisting on this sort of reasoning: "A woman knows when she is getting played. Most women have an intuitive sense."

We certainly have keen intuition. But all too often we second-guess ourselves and avoid the small inner voice that warns us of approaching danger. Well, here are some surefire, telltale signs that will warn you if a player is in the vicinity:

PLAYER DETECTOR: BE ALERT AND EXAMINE HIS WORTH

THE SEVEN INDICATORS OF THE SLICK MANIPULATORS

1. **He's overly charming.** This man is charismatic beyond belief. He has a Ph.D. in "womanology" and has polished his selling pitch so smoothly that he could "sell ice to Eskimos." His goal is to talk you into feeling so special that you'll readily and rapidly jump into bed.

2. **He's a constant flirt.** Whether it's your friend, neighbor, or a stranger, this Casanova shows no respect, remorse, or restraint when it comes to soliciting female attention. He does this in front of you without a second thought, so you can just imagine what he does behind your back.

3. **He's always broke.** His favorite line is "I'm a bit short on funds this week. Can you help me out until I get paid?" The problem is this is a weekly practice, and he makes no

effort to repay the outstanding loans at all. He takes it for granted that you are a cash machine that he can always use for a withdrawal.

4. **He's never ready for a serious commitment.** No matter how romantic and intimate you become, he always classifies you as a "friend." He'll even be bold enough to introduce you to his other female "friends" and constantly remind you that you have no right to get upset because he hasn't made an exclusive commitment to you. (This one has got to go right away, sis. Your body is a treasure, girl—no monogamous contract, no sexual contact!)

5. **He always accuses you of being unfaithful.** This is a sure warning that this man is controlling, possessive, jealous, insecure, unstable, and probably the biggest cheat around. The wise saying, "As a man thinketh, so he is," applies to this player. He wrongfully blames you because he's evaluating you based on his personal value system. There is a 90 percent chance that he's suspicious of you because he's doing the very thing he's falsely accusing you of—cheating.

6. **He's intimidating.** He takes pride in making you feel as if you're lucky to have him. He plays on your subconscious and manipulates you into feeling unworthy, uneasy, insecure, inhibited, and inferior. His game is to condition you to consult with him before you make any and all decisions. He has carved a niche as your personal master. And in actuality the only thing he's truly mastering is the art of manipulation.

7. **He's the crocodile-tear champion.** He will cry buckets of tears just to gain your sympathy and forgiveness. Usually when he's caught in wrongdoings, or in fear of losing you, he will weep on cue. As soon as you turn your back, the tears are gone and he'll carry on with the same trickery and treacherous behavior.

HERE'S THE BEST DEFENSE AGAINST A USER'S OFFENSE

Sis, I couldn't leave you hanging without giving you the 411 on how to kick these tricksters to the curb. You have a gift that, when used properly, no man can outwit. It's called *a woman's intuition.* Some men are wordsmiths and will charm us with the things we like to hear, but deep down inside, your gut instincts will tell you what a person is like from the first to the third date. All too often we ignore the signals because we are determined to make love work. (Girl, been there, done that, ain't going back, and neither should you—you don't have to anymore.) This is what you do to keep game-playing out of your relationship:

1. **Keep it real.** Be up front and insist on honesty. Do not be sucked into an illusion. At the first inkling of any falsehood, distance yourself. If he lies to you, he's going to have to tell several others to conceal whatever he's hiding. If you don't have truth, you can't have trust.

2. **Keep it respectful.** Always maintain your dignity. Anytime anyone tries to belittle your self-worth, he is not worth your time. Go for a man who is kind to you and is a decent citizen in life. Do not be linked with a good-for-nothing, smooth-talking, run-about, careless critter. Place a high value on yourself, sis.

3. **Keep it in proper perspective.** If you know an electric cord has a shortage, don't plug it into the socket. Many men will tell you at the onset that they are already involved with another woman. If they tell you so, believe it. Don't plunge into the affair with the secret notion that you'll eventually win him over into an exclusive relationship with you. Even if it lasts for months or years, usually the way you get a man is the same way you lose him.

SIS YOU DON'T HAVE TO "FAKE IT" TO MAKE IT WORK

Sis, let's be honest with ourselves. We know when someone is not right for us, but we don't want things "to go wrong." I've got news for you: If he's Mr. Wrong, things are bound to go sour rather than sweeter. What's even worse is when we ignore the clear warning signs in the dating period, we drag the dysfunction into the mating and connecting stage, and things become more toxic. If you keep blocking your blessings by wasting your valuable and precious time and emotions on Mr. Wrong, you will never be able to recognize Mr. Right even if he is standing right next to you. You'd have too much internal clutter to hear what he's whispering to your spirit.

This e-mail from an unidentified sister shows that she's definitely sleeping on the "wrong" side of the bed:

Dear Dr. Cornish,

I'm not sure how to address this because it's my first time relating something personal about myself. I am the kind of girl who would like to have a committed relationship with someone I can be intimate with and share my life [with]. But it seems as though I can't make a commitment because I get cold feet when things seem to be getting too serious. Not only that, I don't ever stay in a relationship when my life is being dictated or if I am ever made to feel intimidated.

Recently I started dating a doctor who is a high achiever. He's a very pleasant and down-to-earth guy, but sexually, he's very selfish. It's only what pleases him. Sometimes I feel like a sex slave, and [as if] that's the purpose of me being in the relationship with him. Usually I would just distance myself from the person, but I would like to change the way I approach personal situations. What's your advice?

[signed]
"On the Run"

THIS AIN'T THE ONE, SISTA!

Dear On the Run,

Keep running, not from yourself, but away from this particular "personal situation." It's okay to have the good doctor as a friend, since he's pleasant to be around. But I take it you're hesitant and afraid to talk to him about how you feel regarding his "selfish" bedroom tactic. Girl, it's your body—speak up! First, talk to him and give him a chance to see if he's willing to respect your feelings and your body. The worst thing that can happen is that he decides to get another "sex slave" to misuse. If this is the case, then bid bye-bye to this Neanderthal specimen.

As a matter of fact, this has got to hurt. Why are you putting yourself through this? Sis, you are too important and valuable to be used as a "sperm deposit." Has this "high achiever" talked to you about future togetherness or marriage? There are a lot of underlying issues that have led you to this point. I believe you need to form a strong and healthy personal relationship with yourself first, and then you'll be able to choose a considerate and suitable mate for you.

Looking out for your best interests,
Dr. Grace Cornish

The sister who wrote the following letter has the right idea about reserving her sexuality for her ideal mate.

Dear Dr. Cornish:

I am a twenty-seven-year-old single African-American woman. I am recently divorced and would like to find a decent mate in the future. I would like to date for a couple of years before I remarry. My problem is a lot of guys don't want to court you; they just want to sleep with you and move on. I was glued to *10 Bad Choices* from beginning to end. Some of the most important topics to me were [those] like "[Get the] Affection Before [the] Erection." This brings me to another excellent point you made. You stated that "men are not dogs." Women allow them to be dogs by being intimate with them [too soon] and allowing certain behavior to continue. This is so true. These kind of women have made it hard for women like me.

"Expect your mind to perform any task you ask of it" was also one of my favorite [affirmations]. I truly believe that if a person can visualize where they want to be, they can achieve their goals and make the visualization a reality. Thank you so much for all your inspiration. I have recommended your book to all of my closest friends.

Sincerely,

Vinette

Well, Vinette, you have the right state of mind. I sincerely believe that in a very short while, you'll be connected with your very own healthy soul mate. In the meantime, you can have fun courting and dating, and avoiding the wolves who just want to pounce on you. In order to have a wider selection of decent and available bachelors, you may have to widen your options by crossing a few lines. Two in particular are:

Option 1: Crossing the age line
Option 2: Crossing the color line

OPTION 1: CROSSING THE AGE LINE

Let me get straight to the point: One of the main reasons I find that most sisters keep attracting certain types of men is that they have limited themselves to a small segment of the population by ruling out other types of men. What it really boils down to is most are afraid of what other people will say about any unconventional choices. Very often sisters allow both their love and their lives to be governed by the opinions of families, friends, coworkers, acquaintances, and even strangers.

Let's take the age factor, for example. Generally speaking, a forty-year-old sister would probably not hesitate to date a fifty-year-old man, yet she would wrestle with the idea of dating a thirty-year-old man. One is ten years her senior; the other, ten years her junior. The former ten years is socially acceptable, yet the latter is frequently frowned upon. Why?

One reason is that we have been socially programmed to marry an older and wiser man, who will sweep us off our feet and take care of all our worldly financial needs while cloaking us with father-figure protection. Now, this is a comforting thought and if it becomes your reality, I am in your corner and will cheer you on with a "You go, sis!" from the bottom of my heart. But I will also cheer you on with the same enthusiasm and bravado if you find healthy love with a younger man who brings a smile to your lips and laughter to your life.

And I'm not referring to the younger guy who is looking for momma, or the gigolo "toy boy" who is on the prowl, trying to entrap an older woman to pay his bills—not at all. I'm referring to a healthy-minded and compatible mate, who may just happen to be housed in a body temple some years younger than yours. I've seen many thirty-year-olds who are much more mature, considerate, and goal-oriented than some forty- and fifty-year-olds.

A MAN'S CHRONOLOGICAL AGE DOESN'T
DETERMINE HOW WELL HE'LL TREAT YOU

Sis, it is not written in stone that you have to be linked with an older man. Many older men have been dating younger women for years. Flip the script if you choose. If you're thirty-five or older and reading this, society would expect you to choose a man fortyish or older. There are still many available, kind, mature, and compassionate men in this age category. However, don't limit yourself by ruling out the younger brothers because there are also a lot of forty-year-old men who are already married, and many of the available ones are stuck in their ways. Then there are others who are weighed down with alimony, child-support payments, or going through their "second childhood."

Many sisters have written to me complaining about being disrespected by older men. They initially believed that these men would be chivalrous and much more respectful of their sexuality because of their chronological age and assumed maturity. In many cases, this assumption proved to be untrue. Here's an example:

Dear Dr. Cornish,

I have not had a relationship nor [a] sexual one in over six years. I kept getting myself into bad relationships, so I made a change. I changed me. I started attending school again, found a job, moved out on my own, and traveled. Now, I am thirty years old.

The problem is I am infatuated with an older man who once lived in my building. He told me he was fifty-six, separated, and had been in and out of relationships with younger women. I like him a lot, and we have been friends for five months, however I don't think he wants a *good* and *decent* relationship with me. I feel he wants a casual sexual relationship and maybe to go out to dinner from time to time. I want more than that. I feel I deserve much better.

My reasons for liking him are: he has gentlemanlike qualities; he's a man of the world; he communicates well with me;

he's a father figure. (I'm really not close to my father.) I wish he would just get to know my personality well—meaning my likes and dislikes—and [allow] me [to] get to know him well. I have good intentions concerning him. [But] I feel the relationship will not be right for me, so with your help and my own intuition, I have decided to discontinue my relationship and feelings for him.

Thanks again. You helped [to] spare a person a lot of pain and hurt. I would like to keep the dignity and respect I have for myself.

Sincerely,
Patrice B.

Well done, Patrice. Thank you for sharing. Dating older men does not guarantee a better, more meaningful, or more respectful relationship.

FLIPPIN' THE SCRIPT: THE OLDER
WOMAN/YOUNGER MAN ROMANCE

When Terry McMillan boldly and openly displayed the older woman/younger man relationship in her real life, as depicted in her groundbreaking *New York Times* bestselling book (and the hit movie) *How Stella Got Her Groove Back,* more than a few jaws dropped. When this sister publicly announced that she had met and married her chosen love, a man her junior by several years (approximately twenty), it had two main effects on people across the country. For starters it provoked major gossip, and then it caused a big trend. Many sisters around the country (both Black and White), gained both the courage and the curiosity to test the waters in the open pool of eligible, available, and younger bachelors. All I can say is, go Sister

Terry! Sis, wherever you find happiness, if you're not hurting anybody, or hurting yourself, go for it!

ON THE SPIRITUAL LEVEL, YOU CAN'T LIMIT
YOUR SOUL MATE BY A CERTAIN TYPE

Instead of looking at yourself as a human being with a spirit, view yourself as a spiritual being from God who is having a human experience at this time on Earth. By the way, don't just write this ancient truth off as some new-age philosophy; you were indeed a spirit before you were formed in your mother's womb to become a human body temple. It is very biblical. In Jeremiah 1:4–5, God said, "Before you were formed in the womb, I knew you. And before you were born, I consecrated you."

With that in mind, what if your soul mate, whose spirit is also from the One Living God, happens to be formed and born in a human body temple that is five, seven, ten, or even twelve years after your birth? Take a minute to think about this, sis.

When you throw away previously formed perceptions you'll discover there are a lot more available bachelors than you think. And guess what: All you have to do is choose *one*. I remember years ago, one of my college sister-friends, Nicolette, a five-foot-eight-inch former beauty queen, adamantly refused to date any man under the six-foot mark. Her preconceived idea of the "ideal catch" was "an athletic hunk who would be paid well for playing ball—football, basketball, or baseball would qualify him—as long as he had the height, the muscles, and the billfold." Well, after a whole lot of heartbreaks, shallow relationships, and a completely new outlook on life, she eagerly reports that she has been very happily married to a five-foot-five-inch dentist for over five years and "has since been blessed with two wonderful kids" to complete her healthy marriage.

OPTION 2: CROSSING THE COLOR LINE

Interracial dating is a very touchy subject for many sisters. As a matter of fact, we've read in magazines and observed on national TV talk shows time and time again how Black women are less apt to date interracially than Black men. This is largely due to the mental scars left by the brutal rapes Black women experienced during the days of slavery, and other types of unjust treatment throughout African-American history.

However, we can't ignore the fact that a growing number of Black women are crossing the color line in hopes of finding healthy-minded partners who will love them for who they are. One reason for this is the "eligible-Black-male-shortage" belief. Another reason is the disrespectful treatment some sisters have experienced from Black men in the past. And for others, it's simply a matter of preference.

Every two weeks on the *Queen Latifah* TV talk show (which is no longer airing), we covered topics concerning interracial relationships. I served as the staff psychologist to advise the participants onstage, and I also followed up with after-care counseling at the end of the shows. These programs always yielded high ratings. It's truly amazing that people are so stimulated about interracial relationships—for some, they trigger anger; in others, curiosity; and many have grown to tolerate and accept them.

One of the reasons I find that there is so much anger surrounding this particular issue is the negative way in which Black women are portrayed by the media and by the producers, who are the script writers of these segments. In the first chapter of *10 Bad Choices That Ruin Black Women's Lives,* I gave you a complete exposé of how it was purposely planned to paint an unflattering image of Black women regarding interracial relationships on a now-defunct national TV talk show.

Another national TV show had the audacity to run this caption: "Are you an angry Black woman who wants to confront a Black man for dating outside his race? If you want to say, 'How dare you date only White girls,' give us a call, and you can be a guest on . . ."

Check out the wording, sis. The subliminal message is to put anger in Black women's minds, whether it's there or not.

I must give Latifah her props. Her show lasted for two years, and something like that would never have happened on her show. That sister was a terrific host, who would not stand for any kind of exploitation. (Kudos to you, sister!)

IF YOU CHOOSE TO OPEN YOUR OPTION, YOU'LL HAVE A WIDER SELECTION

I'm the first one to tell you I'm an advocate for beautiful and healthy Black male/Black female relationships. However, I am not, and have never been, against interracial relationships. Let's face facts. We live in a multicultural nation. And it is bound to happen that people of all different backgrounds will relate to one another on some level, and if a healthy love relationship emerges out of some of those associations, then so be it—enjoy the blessings. Let's take it a step further and look at it from the spiritual plane: If we are to hold to the belief that all of humanity emerged from the one God, then so what if

He happens to make us different colors—some white, some black, some red, some brown, and some yellow, etc. What has tarnished humanity is the awful and despicable way we treat each other.

On another show I did, a White woman who was very prejudiced said she "hated" to see Black women/White men bonding, just as strongly as she "hated" the Black men/White women unions. To justify her viewpoint, she said it was written in the Bible that God was against racial mixing and that's why He destroyed the tower and separated the different races in the city of Babel (Gen. 9:1–1).

In a firm but compassionate manner, I told her she was so off the mark to use the Bible to try to validate that awful discrimination: "Don't use the Bible to promote racism and hatred. Let me open the Good Book for you. We are all equal in our Creator's eyes. And surely God destroyed men several times throughout the Bible because of the sinful nature, idol worshiping, hatred, and wickedness we displayed to each other."

I wanted to get further input on this from another viewpoint, so once again, I contacted leading male advocate Dr. James Sniechowski, coauthor of *Be Loved for Who You Really Are.*

DISCUSSING DATING DIFFERENCES WITH DR. JIM

Dr. Grace: What are your thoughts regarding interracial relationships? Oftentimes, there are major differences in culture and religion and these sometimes stimulate anger from outside influences. I sincerely believe that it is good to choose a mate of similar background. We all know, however, that that doesn't ensure a smooth relationship. All relationships take work. In your opinion, how can people

who choose mates of other backgrounds have healthy
unions?

Dr. Jim: First of all, they can't be naive about what they're getting into. Regardless of how we'd all like to think that racial,
religious, and ethnic differences shouldn't matter, we all know
they do. Not just because of racism or bigotry, although that
plays into it as well. But because different groups have different ways of viewing life and coping with the world. Yes, at a
deep level, all of our problems may be the same, but the ways
we relate to them are very different. That means we have different habits that are deep-seated. We have different fears. We
have different preferences.

That doesn't mean that two people from different backgrounds can't make it. Quite the contrary, they can create a
relationship that is much richer, more exciting, more adven-
turesome and more rewarding [than] that [of] those who are
very much alike. They just have to be conscious about what
they're doing.

When two people discover that they love each other and
know that if they marry they will face difficult and sometimes
powerful social obstacles, they should take their differences as
an invitation from God to explore new ways of being. They
can rely on their faith to support them. They have signed up
for a bigger job. They are blessed to be leaders, opening the
world to the truth that we are all brothers and sisters and that
racial or ethnic differences are just a sign of God's profound
creativity.

Great point, Dr. Jim. Sis, love is there for you in whatever
shade, race, or ethnicity you choose. Sure, it will take a lot of
work, but what relationship doesn't? I agree that you share a
certain commonality with a mate of the same racial and cul-

tural background. But having the same skin color does nut automatically guarantee a better bonding. As a matter of fact, two people of different races with similar spirits can be more perfectly matched than two people with the same color yet dissimilar spirits.

However, what's doubly beautiful is two people with similar characteristics and similar spirits. Whatever you choose, sis, "to thine own self be true." Use the following pointers to help you travel smoothly through the dating stage:

The Seven Things You Should Never Do During Any Stage of Dating

1. Don't try to emulate the "type" of woman you were told brothers like to marry.

2. Don't try to act like one of your girlfriends (or a character in a movie, soap opera, or novel) simply because she is always dating.

3. Don't force yourself to fit a particular image based on the kind of woman you believe he would prefer.

4. Don't hold back your true beliefs and personality because you are afraid it might scare him off if you show who you really are.

5. Don't "grin 'n' bear" a distasteful conversation or mannerism if it offends you (politely yet quickly relate your feelings).

6. Don't get swept away by his potential (who he may someday become); instead, deal with the real person staring you in the face.

7. Don't accept another date with him if you're having mixed feelings (it could be your intuition warning you to avoid an unhealthy relationship). Move to the next date until you find the one you would like to have a deeper connection with.

If you follow these guidelines, you will get the respect from the right mate who'll realize, *This woman has a lot of love and respect for herself. Therefore, I have to respect her also. This is the type of woman I deserve and want to be with.*

Keep reading, sis, and find out how to make the soul connection. . . .

connecting with respect has the best effect

Sis, I've got good news for you. Coupling and marriages are on the rise today. This remarkable statistic has evolved from a very devastating and horrific incident that shook up our country and our consciousness on September 11, 2001. The terrorist attacks on the World Trade Center in New York City and the Pentagon in Washington, D.C., on that ill-fated Tuesday morning have left many people with feelings of vulnerability and yearnings to nest with loved ones.

I have done quite a lot of grief counseling for the families and friends of some of the victims and survivors of this tragedy. Needless to say, it has changed many people's views about life, family values, and personal relationships. More and more people are realizing their finite existence on Earth, and realize that they, too, could be gone in a "wink of an eye."

What I found from speaking directly with many brothers is that the 9/11 attack has caused a major shift in their beliefs and views. They are running to the altar to dedicate their lives to one true God, as well as marching down the aisle to dedicate their love to one true woman.

The long three- to six-year, drawn-out engagements are

becoming a thing of the past. As more and more men get in touch with their spiritual selves, more sisters will be walking hand in hand with their very own healthy-minded love. This is your time; claim it, sis.

Another shift that has taken place is that women who would at one time shy away from asking, or think it unfeminine to ask, for a man's hand in marriage have now thrown away the old rule books and are instead following their own intuitions and "popping the question." More and more women are realizing that "life is too short," and are not afraid to go after the healthy love they want and deserve.

What I find especially extraordinary is the substantial increase in the number of singles and couples who are seeking counseling, both spiritual and psychological, in order to mend or remove the differences that have kept them from enjoying deeply connected love relationships in the past. To help shed light on how to overcome differences and form deeper connections, I've decided to tap into the expertise of one of America's favorite husband-and-wife psychology teams, Dr. Jim and Dr. Judith. First, let's hear what Dr. Jim has to say.

CONNECTING THE DIFFERENCES WITH DR. JIM

Dr. Grace: You and your wife, Dr. Judith Sherven, use yourselves as examples in your books and seminars nationwide. You have your differences in your relationship, yet you have a very successful marriage. Can you share an example of how you handle your own differences, and how you create the "connection" that keeps you together?

Dr. Jim: Here is an example of one of our major differences and how we handled it. Judith did not get married until she was forty-four. Her marriage to me is her first and only. During all those years of dating, she developed a powerful fantasy of just how dinner was going to be once she was married. She had imagined dinners with her husband would be lit by candlelight, the table set with beautiful linens and fine china. We would sit at dinner, talking, being together.

But soon after we moved in together, she discovered I was a grazer. I like to snack and munch throughout the day. I did not see anything wrong with a formal, sit-down dinner on special occasions, but I usually ate when I felt like it.

Judith was disappointed and hurt. Her whole fantasy collapsed. I knew she felt bad about what we called our "eating problem," and I was willing to change. But the image of a lifetime of sit-down dinners every day was too much. That was like doing hard time in maximum security.

We knew we had to work this out and respect each other's ways, because this could drive a serious wedge into what we were creating together. We had to really be sensitive and open to new possibilities. But we also knew that if either one of us just gave in, there would be trouble down the line. *We had to find a solution that would be truly satisfying to both of us so that neither one of us felt like [he or she was] losing.* We had to find a way to genuinely appreciate our different eating styles, so we could see them as a chance to learn something new. *That way we would each be the source of discovery and growth for one another.*

PROBLEM-SOLVING 101: "OUT OF THE EATER, CAME THE SWEETER"

When we finally resolved what we called our "eating problem," Judith learned about freedom and flexibility and what fun grazing can be. She also saw how she was caught up in her expectations, her unwillingness to see things differently. If she'd insisted only on her way, that would have ultimately driven us apart.

I had to face my resistance to what felt like being "tied down." My fear of being imprisoned existed only in my own head. When I opened myself and saw how intimate and elegant a formal meal could be, I wanted that.

The basic truth is that we did not try to cope with each other, or manage to tolerate each other. We did not try any technique to solve our problem. *We each listened to one another, openly, with genuine curiosity, and discovered what was valuable about our differences.* That way, we each found value in the other's way of approaching dinner. So our "eating problem" became a path of discovery and change that reached far beyond the surface of how we were going to spend dinnertime together.

DON'T IGNORE, BUT EXPLORE YOUR DIFFERENCES

In closing, Dr. Jim shared this: "My wife, Judith, and I have interviewed thousands of people. . . . Now, we all know that no matter how much two people have in common, when they get into a relationship, they soon discover the many ways [in which] they're different from each other. Yet people are threatened by the differences, so they use them to trash each other. They lash out, damage, and destroy what might be very good relationships.

"Couples fight over anything. The proper way to cut a turkey. Whether or not Aunt Josey should wear that tight dress at her age. How the kids are supposed to be raised. Toothpaste tubes. Toilet paper over the top of the roll or bottom. And, believe it or not, these are the kinds of fights that take people straight to divorce court.

"They are not really fighting over toothpaste. They are

fighting over differences. Whose way is the right way. ´₁
what a power struggle is all about. Each one is trying ₁
his or her own way, because they both believe that the c ₋ᵤ₁
one is ridiculous, stupid, unreasonable, or whatever. That is
how the fear of differences can tear a relationship apart, and
how the two people involved may not even know why."

EXERCISE: Working out the differences: How connected are you with your mate?

The following twelve questions can help you to evaluate and
determine the depth of your present or future relationship. You
can also use them to do periodic spot-checks throughout your
relationship (i.e., every six weeks, every three months, once a
year, etc.):

1. The things I like best about my mate are . . .

2. The things I dislike most about him are . . .

3. He stimulates my interest with ideas and thoughts in the
following ways . . .

4. He does not intrigue me in the following ways . . .

5. He respects, admires, and appreciates my thoughts and
feelings in these areas . . .

6. He fails to respect my thoughts and feelings on these
matters . . .

7. I feel completely at ease and can freely express myself to
him about the following . . .

8. I am uncomfortable and unable to freely communicate
with him about . . .

9. He supports my goals and urges me to pursue my interest in these ways . . .

10. He discourages my dreams, aspirations, and pursuit of
the following goals . . .

11. I enjoy the way he makes me feel when . . .
12. I do not enjoy it when he . . .

After you've completed the above, take some time to really think about each of your responses. Write an overview of your relationship. Then, reverse the roles, and evaluate yourself on his behalf, using the same guidelines. Is your relationship productive and healthy for both of you? Are you happy, somewhat happy, or unhappy most of the time? If there's a major disconnection in your love life, are you both willing to work together to connect the loose ends?

Being truthful when analyzing your relationship will give you a clear picture of your strengths and expose what needs to be worked on in order to solidify your bonding. This way, both of you can sit down, communicate, and find effective solutions that are satisfactory to both of you.

Now, let's hear from the second half of the dynamic duo on creating deeper bonding in our love lives.

SOLIDIFYING THE CONNECTION WITH DR. JUDITH

Dr. Grace: Dr. Judith, you and your husband, Dr. Jim, have helped thousands of couples and singles through your three bestselling books, your seminars, TV–talk show appearances, and your online newsletter. Can you share the formula that connects two people in a healthy relationship?

Dr. Judith: You know, Dr. Grace, the formula is actually quite simple. The problem is that no one receives even basic relationship training for how to date effectively and how to co-create a successful marriage. Instead, we all suffer from unrealistic and misguided fantasies about how it's "supposed" to be, and then when the real thing comes along, we're either not emotionally available to get involved or we spend all time trying to make the other person fit into the fant Here's the formula in a nutshell:

1. Make sure you and your partner are emotionally available for love.

2. Be aware that the first blush of wild romance must fade in order for the two of you to show up more fully for the complexity of a real long-term relationship.

3. Understand that the other person is not you and therefore will have unique ways of thinking, feeling, and expressing himself—different from your ways.

4. Be prepared to negotiate your conflicts so that both of you are satisfied. The changes and challenges you will encounter in marriage are spiritually necessary for the two of you to continually grow in your capacity to love. And it helps you to stay romantic when you understand this.

5. Stay curious about each other, always eager to know about each other's daily events and what the emotional experiences have been.

6. Be affectionate, admiring, and appreciative of one another every day. Do not ever take each other or your love for granted!

REAL LOVE TAKES PLACE IN *REAL* LIFE, WHERE WE *REALLY* GET TESTED WITH *REALLY* BIG CHALLENGES

Dr. Grace: Those are excellent guiding points. You are such a genuine person. What I find fascinating about you is, like me, you practice what you preach. You have a very healthy marriage—the wholesome connection (including the normal ups and downs) that you encourage in others. You are living proof that healthy love works. Most people are deprived of this type of union because they are ready to run when challenges appear. How do couples get the connection going and keep it together when the road gets a little bumpy ahead?

Dr. Judith: Yes, Jim and I have been married fourteen years, and it keeps getting better. And you know that we're both pretty strong-willed, so we've had to really learn how to handle our conflicts in a way that increases our love, rather than tears it apart. That's how "the magic of difference" became the cornerstone of our work.

Sadly, most people do run when the going gets a bit tough. But that is simply a signal that they do not understand the reality of love and what it requires of us. Contrary to the myth that if you meet the "right one" it will be effortless "happily ever after," real love takes place in real life, where we get tested and have to demonstrate that we are worthy of the blessings and benefits that love has to offer.

As I said, the relationship road will necessarily get bumpy. First, two one-of-a-kind people are joining their lives together and they are not going to see eye to eye about everything. Second, old emotional stuff from childhood is going to rear its head and cause trouble from time to time. And third, life is going to deliver some difficult shocks and curveballs, like getting fired, losing a child, an automobile accident, and so on.

TO CONNECT TOGETHER, YOU'VE GOTTA GROW TOGETHER

So the key to relationship success is using these difficult times as opportunities to grow:

1. You need to *grow in your ability* to love each other for who you really are.

2. You need to *grow in your capacity* to receive that kind of deep love.

3. And you need to *grow in your capability* to surrender to where love and life need to take you, so you can be spiritually fulfilled on a daily basis.

Dr. Grace: Beautiful categorizing of the various growth stages! I met you and Dr. Jim at one of your relationship workshops approximately four years ago, and since then we have become good friends. *Ten Bad Choices That Ruin Black Women's Lives* had just been published, and I was teaching a course at the same adult learning center as you were. And out of curiosity, I took your class (and I am so glad I did). I remember observing the silent, yet spiritually visible, oneness that joined you together. I was able to read your signals and body language, and saw that you had deep love and respect for each other, and I remember thinking, "Yes, that's the type of marriage I want and deserve to have someday." (And, I certainly have my very own healthy love relationship right now!) The healthy love and deep spiritual connection between the two of you had a profound effect on everyone in the room, including me. People were intrigued and left there with renewed hope of creating and maintaining their very own healthy relationship. You had a very good effect on me, and that's why I've invited you to share your advice on how to keep the fire burning and make your bond stand the test of time.

Dr. Judith: It was a special moment when we met you in that class in New York City. You were single then, but Jim and I knew, from the way you just beamed positive energy and a zest for living, that you wouldn't be single for long. And now you are co-creating your own spiritually marvelous marriage.

Besides our [Dr. Judith's and Dr. Jim's] respect and value for each other as distinctly different people, which is at the heart of long-lasting love, we make it a point to celebrate being together. Not only do we celebrate the day we met and our wedding anniversary, we also celebrate each other's accomplishments. We compliment each other and offer our appreciation for how wonderful it is to live together. We use private nicknames, and we make love out of bed, touching each other and kissing and hugging . . . just because. This way, the passion between us is kept burning and our love has no chance of withering or becoming boring.

Dr. Grace: In closing, will you share some "girlfriend tips" for sisters reading this, on what women can do to keep their mates intrigued?

Dr. Judith: Having worked with one hundred thousand singles and couples in our trainings, workshops, and private consultations, and listening to the fears and complaints of so many men, it is clear that men want and need love and romance as much as women. However, a man needs to feel that his dignity and identity as a man is safe before he will feel comfortable being emotionally vulnerable with his woman.

He needs to feel safe from being attacked for just being a man, for not expressing himself the way she thinks he "should," for not thinking or planning or feeling the way she does. When a man feels that you care about his well-being, then he will bring himself to you as fully as he knows how.

So let love lead you in the way that you treat your man. Let your desire for your relationship to flourish be the guideline for your actions and reactions. You won't be able to do this perfectly—you are human. But to the degree that you make sure the two of you are on the same team, that's the degree to which you are opening the way for love to continually fill both of your hearts.

Dr. Grace: Amen, and thank you.

A TESTAMENT OF REAL LOVE IN REALLY TRYING TIMES

This sister wrote concerning one matter, but when I read her letter, I had to ask about the joyous way she kept referring to her relationship. Here are portions of both her letters, and my response to the first, so that you can see what I mean.

Dear Dr. Cornish,

I must say [that] I have become increasingly impressed with you, and I finally purchased your book *10 Good Choices That Empower Black Women's Lives.* I LOVE IT. Over the last few years, women like yourself have provided me with so much help and spiritual nourishment.

In the recent past, I've lost two babies, changed jobs five or six times, been estranged and reunited with my family, had plenty of ups and downs with a wonderful man, and started a business. I am growing and learning more about myself every day, yet I find that I am also becoming more and more irritated with negative and bitter people. There was a time when I never talked about my problems and never told people how I really felt.

As I got older, I opened up and did nothing but complain. I thought it was making me feel better, but it was actually [making me feel] worse. Now, I am in the stage of awareness where I am soaking up everything that I can find that is uplifting, enlightening, and nourishing to my spirit and self-esteem. It's good because now I feel as if I have a purpose. But the bad thing is [that] now I am dissatisfied with what I've accepted up until this point. Now that I have started my business (it's not making money yet), I know that I want it to work. I am [currently] in this dead-end job that I absolutely hate. People I used to be close to are now really negative and bitter, and they complain too much. Not that they've changed, but I have, or am trying to (since I have read *10 Good Choices . . .*). I am still hurting from losing my babies, so I've tried to fill up my time and my life with attending school full-time (four to five days per week), working full-time, and running my business. I guess my question is, How do I get past the fear of living my life the way I want to?

I feel people misunderstand me. They don't know that I want positivity and proactivity around me; that I struggle with feeling like a broken woman because I lost my son and second baby; that I want to mentor young women and men, to help them navigate through life; that even though I am in this amazing relationship with a man (four years and counting), it seems like we'll never get married. They don't know how much I struggle with the fear that I may not be good enough to make my business successful. I know I am complaining now. (SMILE.)

I just want to thank you for writing two very much needed books and I feel so much better knowing that there is more to life than just complaining about your circumstances and never doing anything to get past them.

Carmella

Hi, Carmella,

How are you? My assistant just handed me your e-mail. I sometimes get hundreds weekly, but yours stood out because with all you've gone through, you took the time to note how good your relationship is. I promise I will answer your questions [and I have], but I would like to know more about your relationship. Let me explain—I'm currently in the process of researching and writing the manuscript for my forthcoming book, *You Deserve Healthy Love, Sis!,* and I am so fascinated that in your letter you frequently mentioned how wonderful your relationship with your mate is. This certainly sounds like a healthy love match to me, and I would love to use your story in the new book.

I think your story will be a great example for sisters across the globe. If you'd like to be included, please give me a complete rundown on your relationship—don't hold back. Frankly, I'm happy you found a "wonderful" love match. Looking forward to hearing from you.

> With God's blessings,
> Dr. Grace Cornish

Dear Dr. Grace,

I would be more than happy to share with you what we've gone through and how we've been able to make it! I love your books, and I am excited because your e-mail was one of many blessings I received today. His [Carmella's mate's] name is Bradley Anderson, Jr., and I can honestly say that he is the man that I have prayed for. I prayed for someone strong and family-oriented, intelligent, funny, handsome, and strong-minded. He is all of those things and sometimes more than I bargained for. I am twenty-six years old, and he is a very young thirty-seven. People always tell us how we seem to be perfect for each other and that we communicate with each other like we've been together longer than four years. I have always been a fiercely independent, intelligent, yet picky and romantically idealistic [person]. I believe in soul mates, and I was hoping that there was one out there for me.

My younger sister had been fixing me up with a long line of losers, and I had met my share of them on my own. I decided to take a year and just work on me. I started reading self-help books and just spending time with myself. I had to learn what I was putting out there that kept me on the receiving end of pain and suffering. My sister comes to me one day

and says, "I have the perfect guy for you; he works with me."
I told her that I was not in the mood to be put through
another one of her blind dates, and she said, "But this guy is
perfect for you." I was very suspicious about this man,
because my sister and I hadn't been getting along. But I finally
agreed, and she called me at home and then put him on the
phone. I loved his voice immediately, and I actually heard
wedding bells. But I decided not to get excited.

You've got it, sis: A deep connection begins with your mind, not your behind!

We made a date for the weekend, and our conversation
ended. She showed him my picture, and he became suspicious. He thought that a woman as FINE as I was should have
a man. We went to a movie and it was, coincidentally, about
an older man and a younger woman. He was thirty-three at the
time and I was twenty-three. We had a wonderful first date
and talked till 4:00 in the morning. He had to be at work at
6:00 that morning. We ended it with a sweet kiss. Fast-
forward. For those that say a man won't stay if I [a woman
doesn't] don't sleep with him, I want to point out that we
didn't sleep together for three and a half months! He worked
nights and I worked days, but we spent every weekend
together going to different restaurants, movies, and other
wonderfully romantic and fun outings.

A true test of love

Almost one year later, in 1999, we found out that I was
pregnant. I was almost three months along when we found
out. He had just signed a new lease on his apartment, and I
had just moved into a new apartment. He broke his lease and
lost a fifteen-hundred-dollar deposit because he said he felt
the need to be close to me during the pregnancy and I would
need someone to take care of me. I began having complica-
tions and had to be taken to the emergency room. We were

assured that it was probably stress and that I needed bed rest for a couple of days but that the baby was healthy. This happened a few more times, and then a week after my first ultrasound at almost six months of pregnancy, I went into premature labor at my doctor's office.

He [Bradley] drove with me to the hospital, and he was there holding my hand and comforting me for the six hours that I was in labor. My parents were there, but he never left my side and lay across my chest when they pulled the baby out. I was crying and asking my dad if God was punishing me because we weren't married. The pain was excruciating. When everything was over, the nurse came in and asked if I wanted to see my son. I started crying all over again because we didn't know the sex of the baby, and I became hysterical.

He jumped up and told the nurse that he would take care of it. She handed him an envelope, and he left the room for almost an hour. When he came back, he kept kissing my head and telling me that it was okay and thanking me for our son. But he wouldn't tell me about the baby. He said that he would show me the stuff when I was stronger. He stayed with me until I fell asleep, then he went home.

An even greater test of love

They released me the next day, and he came and dressed me, took me out to get something to eat, and to get my prescription filled. He showed me the contents of the envelope maybe a week later. He told me to prepare myself because it would make me cry. In the envelope there were two pictures of our son, his little hat, his I.D. bracelet, and his footprints. [Bradley] told me that he had his eyes and his head, but he had my nose. He said that the baby was still breathing when he left the birthing room, and he wanted to run and tell me that he was alive. But he knew that he wouldn't live long. I felt so empty and hurt at that moment, and he just held me like I was all he had in this world. He took two weeks off from work to grieve and take care of me. Every day after that he changed me, helped me bathe, fed me, and cried with me. We would sit on our balcony for hours just talking about the baby and why it happened.

Connecting on one accord: You feel together, you cry together, you love together . . .

One day, he stayed out all night and when he came in, he just burst into tears. He said that it was his fault because he had done so much wrong in his life. It was my turn to care for him and be strong for him. We talked and I reassured him that he was a wonderful man and that our son would have been blessed to have him in his life. Losing our son brought us together in a way that I can't explain. I felt like we were one person, because at that point he and I were the only two people that felt this particular loss and pain. We had always talked about everything, and we had never argued. This tragedy just reinforced what we had been doing all along.

. . . You talk together, you walk together, you work together

I was out of work for eight weeks and eventually quit because of depression, so he paid the bills, including our two car loans. We didn't have a lot of furniture or spare money, but he still made a way for us to see a movie or have a nice dinner. I kept the house clean between my crying jags and made sure he had a good lunch and dinner to take to work. We became a team. We depended on each other because people didn't call us or come over for whatever reason.

Facing life's most difficult curveballs together

We'd lost our son, Lil' Brad, in September, a few weeks after my birthday, and I was pregnant again in November. I was excited. I felt like God was telling me that everything was going to be okay. Bradley was happy, but restrained. He didn't want to go through the same thing all over again. He said he felt so powerless in the hospital room because I was in so much pain, and he was angry because the doctors weren't doing enough. Unfortunately, I started spotting again and lost the baby in August, a week before my son would've been due. This time was not as bad physically, but I lost a lot of blood and had to have surgery. I also found out that I had two fibroids that may have contributed to the losses. We felt like God had caller I.D. and was ignoring our prayers. It was so unfair and painful.

This time, I threw myself into work. We decided to use birth control and wait to have more children. I started attending school full-time while working full-time. I established a life-skills and career-coaching business, too. We moved to Ohio and decided to start fresh. We found an amazing apartment, and we threw ourselves into decorating it the way we wanted it. [Bradley] bought me a new car before we moved out here because mine had been repossessed. We were beginning to feel happy again. Then something changed. We had all of the material items that we wanted, but we weren't spending any time together.

These are the times when the tests get really tough

We started arguing over little stuff and became very distant with one another. He started spending more time with his friends and working overtime. I started eating and having pity parties. I complained about everything. I became lazy, and our sex life went down the drain. We tried talking, but everything turned into an argument. Money started getting tight, and that added to the tension. I felt neglected and unattractive. He felt lonely and left out. We decided to focus on us, and things got a little better. Then school started again, and we were back at square one. His job was stressing him out. We discovered that he had stress-related asthma and bronchitis. Every time he had a problem at work, he had to be taken to the hospital. We agreed that he should quit his job, and he did.

I thought that it would help him relax and get his health back in order. It was the first time in thirteen years that he had not had a job. This is my first serious relationship, and I did not know that an out-of-work Black man is not easy to deal with. After the first couple of weeks, he became irritable, paranoid, angry, and sad all the time. He wasn't feeling productive, and he was taking it out on me. He started hanging out with his friends all night, he stopped working out, and again our sex life flew out the window.

Disconnect the naysayers from your love life

People kept asking us when we were getting married and telling us that we were going to hell for living together. I started listening to bitter women, and I was becoming bitter as well. They were telling me that we didn't have a real relationship and that [Bradley] was not committed to me. They said that he was taking advantage of me and that I needed to leave him because we weren't going to get married. I took it out on him because I believed what they were saying. I felt like he was just using me to get away from his family. It was hard. I honestly thought it was over, and it hurt me to no end. We had been through so much with our families, with losing the babies and him not working. But I decided that maybe it was for the best that we split up.

From painful tests to gainful testimony

But something happened at the end of 2001, and he came to realize that he was wrong about a lot of things. He came to me after a particularly severe argument and apologized from the bottom of his heart. He said that I was his world and that he never wanted to lose me. He promised me that he would be a better man to me and for me. He said that we would get married as we had been planning and that he was going to start spending quality time with me the way we used to. He asked me to forgive him for all the things he had done lately. He said that he wanted to take care of me for the rest of my life and that he wanted to spend the rest of his life with me.

Communication is a crucial key for connecting with your soul mate

I guess, to summarize this, we communicate with each other no matter what is going on. He loves me with everything that is in him, and I reciprocate. He is fiercely protective of me and of our relationship, and we are dedicated to making this work at all costs. We recognize the times when we take each other for granted, and we appreciate each other. We are learning to give each other space. There are times when we make each other's teeth itch (SMILE) but we know that in the end, we need one another and want to be together. I have come to a point in my life where I am not going to apologize for or justify my relationship with him to anyone. We are working on us so that when we do get married, we can enjoy each other. I know it'll be hard work, but we've had a lot of tests already, and we made it through those. There are still people out there that doubt us and proceed to dog our relationship, but I am strong enough today to ignore them. Thank you for giving me the opportunity to tell my story.

Carmella

CONNECTING IS MORE THAN JUST A RING THING

Thank you, sis. I love this story! I believe Carmella has truly connected with her soul mate. I am positive that she and

Bradley will set their wedding date in the very near future. A wedding is meant to be a beautiful and important ceremony to top off your love, and the both of them very much deserve to have one.

Do you know that there is a deep connection between a spiritual marriage and a physical wedding? Sis, the ultimate goal of healthy love is not necessarily about getting a ring to form a circle around your finger for the world to see, but to get an ideal mate to form an eternal circle of love around your heart for you both to feel. The spiritual marriage begins long before you say, "I do." It is a deep connection that two people share in a monogamous, loving, and respectful relationship. The wedding is an outward celebration, a symbol to declare to the rest of the world, "This is my soul mate whom I have chosen to spend the rest of my life with." A ring or a marriage certificate without healthy love and respect to go along with it is a counterfeit connection. That false bonding will eventually come to a halt. Here's one sister's testimony:

Dear Dr. Cornish:

I am an attractive forty-four-year-old black woman who has experienced more than my share of bad relationships. Reading *10 Bad Choices* was a Godsend; I truly believe that because I recently came out of a six-year relationship with a man who did not want to commit to me. He bought me two engagement rings (to pacify me), yet would never set a date. I truly believe that reading your book has given me insight and helped me point out areas that I need to explore in myself so that I can make better choices in the future. Once again thank you so much for writing this book!

Sincerely,

Glenda P.

P.S. The blue-collar brother in chapter 2 (Winston), is he still available? I would love to converse with him (smile). You never know.

HOW TO KNOW IF YOU HAVE FOUND THE ONE

You are welcome, sister Glenda. Good for you for releasing that unhealthy-minded, commitment-phobic, time-consuming, ex-fiancé from your personal space. He was only buying time by buying you two rings. Let's face it, what sister wouldn't like to sport beautiful engagement and wedding rings on her fingers? I can surely identify with that. However, sis, I cannot emphasize enough, it's not just about the rings, but more so about what the rings represent—those sacred circles are symbolic of a lifetime of unbroken love that connects two souls together. If one of the two souls is hesitant to walk hand in hand with the other, then they are not soul mates, but instead, two mismatched souls temporarily mating—buying time—until either or both wake up to the reality that they have not yet found "the one."

I promised to shared my personal story with you, so here it is. My soul mate happens to be a few years younger than I, and a few digits more financially secure than I. In my opinion, he is a mature, gorgeous, and intelligent chocolate hunk! (That's just the healthy love beaming out of me, sis.) Honestly speaking, these characteristics had nothing to do with my decision to marry him. As a matter of fact, I met him two years before I started dating him. For me, it was a spiritual-growth process, although as he tells it, he *knew* it was love at first sight for him.

A few months after we were married, I asked Richard how

he knew that I was "the one" from the first time he had met and spoken with me and that it wasn't infatuation instead of love prompting him on. This is how he answered: "Honey, I knew because lust speaks to a man through his penis, while infatuation speaks to him from his mind for a short while. But when I met you both my heart and my mind were speaking the same language, at the same time, from the very beginning. My heart was speaking directly to my mind, and has not stopped since. And to be certain, I also prayed to God for guidance."

Sis, talking with him is like talking to the mirror reflection of myself. He has an old soul, and I have a young spirit; put us together, and you have one healthy love match—spiritually, mentally, and physically. We share a good connection—we are very happy and comfortable with each other, and people are always asking, "You two look so much alike, are you sure you're not related?"

Well, we are now.

PRAYER PLAYS A PROFOUND PART...

One of the best connecting tools you can have is prayer. Yup, some good old-fashioned prayer. It really works. Ask God to remove all the jokers from the deck and give you a discerning spirit to spot and avoid the cunning characters. You know what? When I prayed for *a husband,* I got three proposals in a one-year period. On the surface, they were all great possibilities. I received the first proposal from a very handsome psychotherapist whom I had known for almost eight years. When he popped the question, I told him I would think about it. One of my girlfriends exclaimed, "Girl, that's a good catch! I wouldn't let him get away." My response was "I know he

would be a terrific mate for somebody, but I'm not
belong together." He kept insisting. But I had to pr
because although I was attracted to him and was f..
his proposal, I wasn't feeling strongly about him in my spirit.

...BUT YOU'VE GOTTA BE SPECIFIC WHEN YOU ASK

You won't believe who the second one was from. Have you
already read *10 Bad Choices?* Well, remember Daniel, on page
185, my college fiancé whom I included in the section about
"looking internally to correct problems externally"? After fifteen years of not seeing each other, he got my number from
the Internet, and we spent time talking and catching up about
events over the years. He had been married and divorced and
was currently in private practice as an anesthesiologist. And
again, when he popped the question, I prayed. So this time, I
had a soul-stirring, heart-to-heart talk with God, and instead
of praying for *a husband,* I asked for *my husband.*

Then came Richard. Actually I had met him two years
before when he was visiting New York. He was a geologist
and a well-established business owner in Jamaica, West
Indies. His reason for being in New York that July was to visit
his ailing dad, with whom he shared a very close father-son
bond. His brother and sister-in-law and I were friends, and
one day they all stopped by to visit me. Richard and I saw each
other a couple of times before his five-week trip was cut short
by his father's death. I thought he was handsome, but I never
entertained the thought of a relationship at that time because
I was very happy being celibate, married to my career, and
about to move to my new home in the South. I honestly had
no clue that he was remotely attracted to me. I wasn't looking
for it, so I didn't see it. We just got along really well.

SOMETHING TO THINK ABOUT, SIS: YOU COULD'VE ALREADY MET YOUR SOUL MATE, BUT HAVEN'T RECOGNIZED HIM YET!

During that two-year span, I had given many seminars and had received many awards on the island of Jamaica. But each time I was there, Richard was either lecturing on some other neighboring island, doing research at the University of the West Indies, or teaching chemistry and geology.

Anyway, we had no direct contact until I had my soul-stirring heart-to-heart with God. After eighteen months, I had moved back to New York. I had accepted the offer to be the "after-care and staff psychologist" for the *Queen Latifah* TV talk show, and I had also enrolled in seminary full-time. It was right before Christmas that I had opened my heart to heaven and prayed for *my husband,* and within a month (I'm not kidding you, sis)—by mid-January—Richard's brother confessed, "You know, my brother is in love with you. Every week we speak on the phone, the first thing that comes out of his mouth is, 'How's Grace?' I haven't given him your new number, and I have never told you about his feelings because you're such a busy career woman, I figured you'd have no time for any relationship at this point in your life."

IF YOU WANT THE BEST, PUT IT TO THE ULTIMATE TEST

Sis, my comment was "What's his number?" I had no hesitation about calling. And when I spoke and reconnected with Richard, after not seeing him in almost two years, I immediately felt he was "the one." We had so much in common, it was almost scary. I would start a sentence, and he would finish it; he would start, and I would finish. But to put our relationship to a deeper test, three months later, I prayed again, and I asked the Holy Spirit to reveal the truth to me. My prayer consisted of three things:

1. God, above all, he has to love you first and foremost.

2. Next, he has to have no emotional baggage and have a healthy sense of self.

3. Then, he has to be able to love me as much as he loves himself.

BE CAREFUL WHAT YOU ASK FOR; YOU MIGHT JUST GET IT!

No one but God knew this personal prayer of mine. Sis, hold on tightly to this book, because when the Holy Spirit moves, it moves. Get ready for your personal blessings—I'm living proof this stuff really works. It's real! Guess what—around two weeks after saying my prayer, I was lying on my couch when Richard confessed, "Grace, I have to share something with you. I couldn't love you if you were not a God-fearing woman. Because God is the guiding force in my life, and I love Him more than anything or anyone. I have had a good upbringing, and I have no self-esteem problems. I like my life and love myself. But the very breath in my body, I love you just as much."

Plop! I fell off my couch! I hit the floor and reality hit me. At that exact moment, I *knew* he was the one. My very own soul mate. Finally, I had met and recognized the man whom I would spend the rest of my life with.

A couple of months after, one of my friends called me to ask, "How do you know he's the one?"

"Girl, all I can tell you is I have never felt this much love for a man before, and had a man love me so much at the same time. It's a spiritual trip. All I can say is it feels as if we are kindred souls. It's as if God is holding a golden cord in the palm of His hand from heaven, and one end of the string is attached to Richard's belly button, and the other end is fastened to mine."

"That's amazing," she remarked. "That should be part of your wedding vows." We were married a few months later.

POLISHING YOUR CONNECTION: THAT MAGIC TOUCH OF HEALTHY, CREATIVE SEX

There is no way I could expect to talk to you about creating and maintaining a wholesome and healthy relationship without addressing the topic of sex. I do believe that the most deeply connected relationships are those in which you first meet spirit to spirit, then mind to mind, and then top it off by intertwining body to body. In this book, I've laid out a well-designed plan for you to attract your soul mate by following the steps herein. I hope by the time you get to the sex stage, you and your mate will have already vowed to have a monogamous relationship with each other, and already formed a lasting bond of respect and love.

It is a popular belief that the urge for love is one of the most powerful of female emotions, while the urge for sex is one of the strongest of male emotions. Generally speaking, while many women may share sex in hopes of receiving love, men may share love in hopes of receiving sex. The emotional urge for sex is a natural part of our equilibrium—there is nothing to feel ashamed about. However, if abused, it becomes greedy, dirty, and corrupt. Sex is a wonderful, important, and enjoyable component of romantic-love relationships. If nurtured in a healthy love union, it becomes more compassionate, more sustaining, more spiritual—it becomes more *deep*.

For eons, people have been obsessed with sex. There have been many ancient cultures whose religions, such as some Roman and Greek sects, encouraged sex openly. Western religions, however, from the eighteenth century on, had repressed sex. But in modern civilization, after many years of repression, people had become rebellious, and instead of sexual repression, *sexual obsession* had become the new code of conduct. Both are extreme behaviors, both are harmful.

This rebellion can be dated back to "the roaring" 1920s and was catapulted to a pinnacle at the onset of the 1960s, where "Free will for free sex" was the motto of the day. As we traveled through the 1970s, '80s, and '90s, all the way to the twentieth-century finish line, we can see the results of the out-of-control sex acts by the astonishingly high figures of sexually transmitted diseases, AIDS, unwanted pregnancies, and cyberspace porn, to name a few.

NOT JUST A "SEX THANG"

The new millennium seems to have ushered in a new awareness of purpose along with a new regard for pursuing a higher and healthier form of love—a bonding between the mind, body, and spirit. More and more people are embracing sex as a part of a "nest-'n'-couple" union, instead of a "hit-or-miss" romance. It can be safely argued that women are farther ahead in their pursuit of the former than their male counterparts. However, to put it in layman's terms, the brothers are getting with the program and seeking healthy love relationships, too.

Generally speaking, people have sex for three reasons:

1. *Procreation*—to continue the human race
2. *Accommodation*—to feel wanted by satisfying another
3. *Recreation*—to have orgasms

If you were to ask ten different people their reasons for having sex, you'd most likely get ten different answers.

However, each answer would fit within the three categories above. Test it for yourself. Take a few minutes to think about it. The first two are basically self-explanatory. Let us look into the third—recreational sex to have orgasms.

By the way, sis, you don't have to blush or feel embarrassed here because I have received numerous complaints from too many sisters who have confided that they have faked orgasms in an attempt to please their mates, yet they themselves are unfulfilled and unhappy. This is not *making the connection;* it is *missing the connection.* In the epilogue of *10 Bad Choices,* I talked briefly about women bluffing orgasms, and it opened up a whole new level of conversation. I have received too many inquiries to answer all individually, so here is my overview of this "hush-hush" topic.

KEEPING IT REAL: IT'S A NATURAL PART OF YOUR CONNECTION, SO STOP FAKING IT!

An orgasm is the natural rising of the vibrations of the human system to meet the need of the body impulses. This is induced by mental, physical, and/or visual stimulation. When it reaches the highest level, the peak, the climax, your thinking stops. At this exact moment, you are completely absorbed in the experience. This is the point of ecstasy, or pure bliss. Because you become so deeply emerged in the experience, you are unable to concentrate. Sometimes it may seem like an explosion, or fireworks, but your mind is actually blank; you experience perfect harmony. At this therapeutic moment, you become completely uninhibited, completely free, and completely fulfilled.

It is because of moments like these that sex, the stimulant, is one of the strongest of male desires. So powerful is this desire that relationships are either strengthened or weakened by it. For example, there are many people who are not properly suited for each other, but because of *good sex,* they stay together. Then there are those who are compatible in many areas, but due to lack of *good sex,* they are torn apart.

BE WILLING TO GROW AND EXPLORE WITH YOUR SOUL MATE

Can you count the number of times you've heard stories, or have seen me give counseling on TV talk shows about men who have been married to beautiful, loving, and devoted wives for years and then one day decided to trade in all they had accomplished together with their spouses for another woman? Or about the many, many men who, on the surface, look like ideal husbands, mates, or family men but secretly keep mistresses, or have extramarital affairs or one-night stands with women ranging from exclusive call girls to common street prostitutes? Whether these men are princes, paupers, or politicians, the results are the same. Unless they have psychological problems, they are cheating for the physical sex. Not just for the act of sex, but for the *creativity* of sex. Creative, recreational sex is a wonderful part of a healthy love union and keeps your bonding fresh, interesting, and new.

Don't fake it, sis. Instead, strengthen your connection by communicating openly and honestly with your present or future soul mate about his likes and dislikes. Let him know your desires and discomforts as well. Find out what turns him on. *Do not* do anything that makes you uncomfortable, but be willing to grow and explore together in your union. I cannot emphasize enough how very important it is for you to be sexually aware, because many men are hypocritical with their mates. They'll place their mates on pedestals, and expect them to act saintly, but then these very same men indulge in *creative* sex with other women. This double standard is very dishonest and unfair, but it is many times a reality. A lot of men are so wrapped up with creative, recreational sex, that they voluntarily risk their reputations and lives for it. Now, sis, these are the particular men that you have to avoid.

IT'S NOT THE *QUANTITY,* BUT THE *QUALITY* THAT COUNTS

Frankly speaking, sis, never compromise yourself to your own discomfort; learn to be a "lady" in the open, but behind closed doors, become *creative* with your soul mate. It's not necessarily the *quantity* of sex, but the *quality.* Most men don't stray because they want more sex; they stray because they are searching for a romantic and refreshing connection.

During an episode of a popular TV talk show on the topic "Why Do Men Cheat?" one fellow proudly shared, "If a man eats steak every day, he'll get bored. He'll sometimes want to try chicken or fish." Although his terminology for women may have been distasteful, the overall statement is very true because of the human desire for *creativity* and *newness.* However, sis, there are many creative ways to prepare steak, with new and invigorating ideas. Feed him new dishes with an ongoing menu of original and exciting herbs, spices, and garnishes—as he in turn should do for you. I read in the Bible that "the marriage bed is undefiled." Well, hello there—when tastefully prepared, steak will become so satisfying to your mate that any desire to sample chicken or fish will become an appetite of the past. (Amen to that!)

CONNECTING WITH THE CONTEMPORARY BROTHER

In December 2000, *Ebony* magazine published the results of the first survey taken of their male readers in order to provide us with a peek into the mind-set and feelings of contemporary brothers. The results were formulated from the answers provided by over one thousand Black men. The article, "What Black Men Really Want," challenged and corrected many of the assumptions that have been accepted about Black men and their sexuality.

Contrary to popular belief, the findings reported that brothers were basically monogamous, most were generally faithful to their wives and lovers, and over 50 percent declared that they had never cheated on their mate. The survey also shared that today's Black men were willing to help with domestic tasks, and almost 80 percent dismissed the notion that a woman's complexion influenced their decision when considering marriage.

In regard to sex, this is what was reported: "While two-thirds of the respondents described themselves as being somewhat sexually experimental, these guys are far from being an oversexed lot. They were almost evenly divided on the topic of premarital relations, with nearly 40 percent saying they would marry a woman with whom they'd not been intimate and 41 percent saying they would not."

There you have it, sis. A confirmation that contemporary brothers are much more monogamous than we once believed. Just as they're inclined to remain faithful to the woman of their choice, there is also an increase of women taking the initiative and proposing to the man of their choice.

TO ASK, OR NOT TO ASK; THAT IS THE QUESTION.

An article in *Ebony* magazine, "How to Propose to Your Man," reported, "For eons, men had complete control over whether and when to say the four words that so many women long to hear. But not anymore. Today many sisters are challenging the status quo by getting down on their knees and asking Mr. Right for his hand in marriage." The article revealed that this growing yet quiet practice of contemporary sisters has become as popular as the Sadie Hawkins Day tradition—the one day in a leap year when women are encouraged to propose to their men. The article also stated that "Although the increasingly widespread practice of women-led proposals may raise a few eyebrows, more and more women are getting exactly what they want—a new husband or a clearer picture of where their relationship is (or is not) headed."

Sis, this is a very personal decision. This is one of those situations that differs with each relationship. I suggest that you weigh this up and pray about it thoroughly before popping the big question. Do what I did; ask the Holy Spirit for guidance, and if and when you get the go-ahead, then go for it with confidence and joy. On a higher spiritual level, when you pray and open yourself to receive a direct answer from God, it will come. You'll know if he's the right one, but you have to be willing to pay attention to the still small voice within.

When Richard popped the question, I immediately said yes. I didn't have to pray and ponder any further about him as I had with the two prior proposals because I felt a deep spiritual connection with him. We seemed so much in sync with each other that if he hadn't asked me, I felt so comfortable and in tune with him, I believe I would have eventually asked him. So, sis, it depends on you, and on the beliefs of the man you are involved with. A lot of men will welcome the idea, but many are still very traditional and old-fashioned and believe it is the man's responsibility to ask for the woman's hand in marriage. However, if he's really your soul mate, you don't have to worry because you both will be vibrating to the same frequency, and reading each other's signals. If you decide to propose marriage, do so with honesty, and avoid doing it for any of the following reasons:

The Seven Reasons Not to Propose

1. Do not propose because you are longing for a ring on your finger.

2. Do not propose because you feel that your biological clock is ticking.

3. Do not propose because family and friends are pressuring you.

4. Do not propose because you feel you have to nab him before anyone else does.

5. Do not propose because you feel that he owes you for all the years you invested.

6. Do not propose because you want to be labeled Mrs. So-'n'-So.

7. Do not propose because your friends are getting married and you feel left out.

Instead, propose because you are absolutely sure that this is the man you want to spend the rest of your life with because he looks out for your best interests, loves you for who you are, enriches your life, and would love to spend the rest of his life with you also.

GOING FOR THE PROPOSAL

Sis, I'm sure in many of the stories about proposals you've heard and read, married women talk about how their husbands either got down on one knee or slipped an engagement ring in a glass of champagne and romantically asked them to spend the rest of their lives with them.

Many are true, but many are not. Very rarely does the

woman talk about how she used her wits to prompt the man of her dreams to pop the question, and even more rarely will she admit that she planned and initiated the proposal. I don't think this is anything to be ashamed of; I think it's smart.

I think it's smart because marriage is not a mysterious arrangement that you blindly step into. As a matter of fact, two people are in a sense already married if they act and bond like an ideal couple. For instance, if you are in a monogamous relationship with each other, you spend all your available time together, you enjoy each other, you understand and communicate well, and you live as if you belong exclusively to each other, then you are basically married to each other. But it is not legally or morally completed until you sign a written contract with each other, and have witnesses standing in on your behalf. Therefore, sis, if you're together for at least six months to one year and living as if you're already married, then it's time to pop the question. Sometimes the brother may need a little prompting—so if he doesn't propose, then there is nothing wrong with your popping the question to your exclusive mate.

Here's a delicate way to handle it. Be sincere, and share this with him: "Sweetheart, we enjoy each other so much, wouldn't it be great to be like this forever? I wish most people could be as happy as we are. I don't want us to ever lose each other. What do you think about us getting married?"

Pay attention to his answer and body language. Some men will say yes right away; others may need time to think about it. If he needs time, give him room to think. Never issue an ultimatum. However, if he says no, and hasn't any intentions of ever marrying you, then you need to decide if you want to spend any more of your precious life with someone who is temporarily renting your affection instead of permanently investing in your well-being. If you have a strong connection, you have nothing to worry about, sis. The best time to ask is usually between Thanksgiving and Christmas because the holiday season promotes a feeling of family ties and togetherness. If your mate asks what would you like for your Christmas gift, answer, "Honey, I want *you* for my permanent present." Don't remark that you want "a ring" or "a wedding," because that may come across as wanting the material instead of his true essence.

A lot of proposals also take place on Valentine's Day because of its romantic flavor. However, your heart, head, and intuition will tell you when it's best to pop the question. Pop it when you feel it, no matter what day or time of the year. If you have made a true connection with your mate, then by all means, pray for it, and go for it!

learn to affirm healthy love in your life

O kay, sis, listen up—we have seen and heard count-less stories about Black women and bad relationships and marriages. God knows, I get a bevy of e-mail on a daily basis that attests to this unfortunate condition. If you add this to the dull picture of Black relationships that is often painted by mainstream media and pop culture, sisters may wonder if there are any signs of healthy love out there.

Sure there are! And more than you may think. Thank goodness for Black magazines, books, and recent Black films that provide us with inspiration and insight into healthy and happy Black relationships. When I was rounding off the research for this chapter, I wanted to make sure I provided you with accurate information that can help you realize how great your possibilities are for attracting and enjoying a healthy love relationship with a wonderful Black man in this lifetime. What better way to affirm this reality, thumb your nose at negative statistics, and ignore naysayers than to find sisters just like you and me who are currently enjoying healthy love relationships, and have them share their stories and ideas.

SISTAS HELPING SISTAS

I sent out a preliminary survey via the Internet to sisters, asking them to talk about their relationships, and the first batch of responses was good. But when I sent out a second survey, eight weeks after the first, and one week following the 9/11 tragedy, I wasn't quite prepared (but was very delighted) for the remarkably large number of positive and happy letters from sisters all over the country who have been enjoying healthy love relationships and marriages with fantastic Black men. Sorting through the letters was a pleasant task. The sisters shared many interesting ways in which they had met and married their soul mates. Some met through mutual friends, blind dates, personal ads, on the Internet, at the workplace, or in the process of pursuing a hobby that interested them.

The following stories will provide an inspiring and refreshing look into the hearts and lives of sisters who are presently happily married to their very own chocolate soul mates. They will discuss openly joys and challenges about getting married and making it last. Many of them will touch on the points I've made throughout this book. More important, they will serve as seasoned marriage counselors and provide tips that you'll find useful in creating and maintaining a healthy and long-lasting union with the man whom you love. When you finish reading their stories, you'll want to turn to your close girlfriends for their support and guidance as you develop your own healthy relationship.

ANNIE: THE MAILMAN WILL DELIVER IF HE HAS YOUR CORRECT ADDRESS!

Annie was thirty-seven and Sam was thirty-eight when they got married five years ago. They were both postal workers, who had met and worked together for eight years at the same office in Brooklyn, New York, before they started dating.

"Twice a month, a few of us used to go out for drinks after work on Friday evenings," Annie shared. "Sam was always a chatterbox after a few beers. After the first three months, we had become very good friends, but there wasn't a physical attraction for either of us. We just weren't each other's type, and we were both seeing other people. We had our share of relationship problems, and would talk about them at our Friday-night get-togethers. Even when we both broke up with our various lovers throughout the years, we never got together in between relationships. We were friends, and it never occurred to us to date each other. Besides, I had made a promise to myself that I would never get married to a postal worker because I was looking for a brother who was finan- cially well-off, and that excluded any of the mailmen I knew. That's probably why I never thought of Sam as a dating pos- sibility."

Well, at least not until her thirty-sixth birthday, when Sam invited her out on a real date to celebrate her special day. They were married exactly one year later.

"We still laugh about how ironic it is that for eight years of working together and hanging out with the gang on Fridays, we never felt any romantic sparks toward each other. Yet, we were instantly and magnetically drawn to each other on our first real date alone. That same evening we both knew with- out a doubt that we were destined to be together forever," said Annie. "The things that I liked about him are the same characteristics that he has always possessed—Sam is very humble yet talkative, honest, funny, kind to others, and always a gentleman."

A GOOD SENSE OF HUMOR IS ALWAYS A WINNER

"Let me tell you how funny he is. When he proposed during our fourth month of dating, I jokingly said that I like big things, and I would love to have a diamond the size of an onion. Since we were already great friends, he knew that I was only kidding. But the following week, he gave me a medium-sized Tiffany's box with a pretty white satin bow." Annie laughed. "Inside, I found an onion with a cute note that read, 'If you marry me, my Nubian princess, someday I'll buy you a diamond the size of an onion.'

"I haven't gotten an onion-sized diamond yet, but we went shopping together, and picked out a nice and affordable ring that we both liked. I love my Sam. I had met many brothers while dating—some with large bankrolls—but none of them can match what we share together. It's funny that I wound up marrying a man who had been under my nose all this time."

Annie's situation reflects that your Nubian Prince Charming and future hubby may be much nearer to you than you think. Talk about overnight delivery!

CHRISTINE: DON'T BE MISLED BY APPEARANCES

Christine was an independent sister in the midst of building her career as a makeup artist in the entertainment industry in Los Angeles. She hardly had time to unplug and unwind from her busy schedule, much less to take time out to find and date a worthwhile Black man. The men she came across in her profession were either "too blond" for her taste or "weren't interested in [her] gender at all." Meeting anyone at work was not an option for her. Therefore, somewhere in the back of her

mind, she entertained the notion that whenever time permit-
ted, she would meet and marry "an exciting, fun-loving,
buffed, chocolate-skinned brother who didn't have to be
wealthy, but had to be able to support himself."

She shocked her friends, relatives, and herself when she did
something at thirty-seven she had pledged she would never
do—she married Ed, "a forty-five-year-old, low-key, conservative, slightly chubby, light-skinned Black man."

"My family was surprised, yet very delighted that I was
finally getting married," she said. "Especially my mother. My
younger sister, Joan, thirty-two, had gotten married three
years before, and my family had always been on my case. They
live in Dallas, Texas, and one of the reasons I moved to
California was to get away from their probing questions, gos-
siping tongues, and overbearing stares all the time. At family
reunions and gatherings I was always the main topic dis-
cussed. Many of them whispered that I was the 'old maid' in
the family. But I didn't care. I loved my career, and I was not
going to rush into something just to make everyone else
happy. I knew it would happen when I was ready.

"They knew that I was the free-spirited, fun-loving, and
easygoing type, so you can just imagine how shocked they all
were to find out that I was 'finally settling down' with a quiet
and conservative man. But they were even more thrilled when
they discovered that he was a judge, and a rich one at that."

SOMETIMES YOU NEVER KNOW WHAT PLEASANT
SURPRISES LIFE HOLDS

While Christine was putting herself through cosmetology
school and interning on various movie sets, she worked as
Ed's secretary for six years. At age thirty-three she left to enter
the cosmetics world full-time. She had a lot of respect and

admiration for her former boss. They had become good friends, and she kept in touch periodically.

"He was great to work for," she recalled. "We got along well. Although I always thought he was good-looking, I never entertained any romantic notions about him because not only was he a married man with two teenage kids, he was just too conservative and too light-skinned for my taste."

For two years, Christine was immersed in the fast-moving entertainment field. She was enjoying her chosen profession. Then one day, an ex-coworker and good friend called her from Ed's office to tell her that he and his wife were splitting up and ending their marriage. She was very surprised by that news, because she knew how traditional he was and how important family values were to him. She called to offer him her sympathy. He was appreciative, and instantly she became a sounding board for his regrets about having to adjust to living on his own and learning how to exist on fast food.

THE WAY TO SOME MEN'S HEARTS IS STILL
THROUGH THEIR BELLIES

After having come home and been greeted by his weekly messages on her answering machine, Christine decided to invite Ed over to have a full-course, Texan-style home-cooked meal. He accepted. He enjoyed both her cooking and her company. She didn't realize that he was getting romantically attached to her when he complimented her on her attractive looks and good cooking in his adorable yet quirky comment "Lookers usually aren't cookers. You're a special woman and have a lot of admirable qualities." After sampling her cooking, he became a regular dinner guest on her days off.

"We got to know each other so much more over the next few months," Christine shared. "But I never wanted him for myself. As a matter of fact, one evening over a glass of wine, he loosened up, and I started to give him tips on how to reconcile with his wife. After a second glass of wine, he confessed, 'We got married too early—we were barely out of our teenage years. We were both miserable because we really didn't belong together. She was pregnant when we got married, and we stayed together because of our children. We agreed that when the kids got old enough to go off to college, we would divorce. In a way, it's a relief for both of us.'"

The following week, Ed asked Christine to go out with him. But she refused because she didn't want him to think that they were dating as a couple. Although she enjoyed him as a friend, she made it a personal rule of hers not to get intimately involved with either conservative or light-skinned men. She had a personal preference for dark-skinned brothers.

"This really surprised and disturbed him," observed Christine. "He said, 'I don't get it. We enjoy each other's company, don't we? You could be polka-dotted and it wouldn't affect the way I feel about you. I am neither turned on nor turned off by your dark skin—it really doesn't matter to me. I am falling in love with you because of who you are and how comfortable I feel with you. I like being with you.'"

At that moment, Christine saw a different side of Ed. She said that's when she realized that she was rapidly falling in love with him also. Ten months after that, they were engaged. Eight months later, they wed, and have been happily married for seven years.

"The biggest lesson for me was to get rid of my stereotypes regarding Black men," confessed Christine. "I always stayed away from the conservative ones, because I always thought they would be stuck-up. It just goes to show that we can never *judge* a book by its cover. No pun intended. Who knew that the love of my life would be a conservative judge, wrapped in the very package that I used to turn away from."

Well said, Sister Christine. We've got to keep open minds and to open ourselves to greater possibilities.

KARLA: BE WILLING TO TRAVEL BEYOND YOUR DEMOGRAPHICAL AREA

To make her very own healthy love connection, twenty-seven-year-old Karla had to travel into some unfamiliar territory. Her first date with thirty-one-year-old Rodney was one of those wake-up calls that require you to go with your gut feelings and ignore the supportive but suspicious advice of family and friends.

Karla was a product developer for a toy-manufacturing plant in Minneapolis, Minnesota, when she met Rodney, a military officer stationed in Norfolk, Virginia, in a live chat-room online.

"After corresponding in two of the group sessions online, we connected because we had a lot in common," Karla remarked. "At first we e-mailed each other back and forth every day for three weeks. Then we decided to exchange phone numbers. When I found out where he lived, I was a little hesitant to go any further because I have never traveled outside of the state of Minnesota. However, I really enjoyed talking with him, and looked forward to getting to know him more. It was a big surprise to find a Black man who was really interested in a Black woman. In Minneapolis, just about 99.9 percent of Black men date and marry White women. I'm not exaggerating. You have to see it to believe it. I don't know what it is, but the Black men where I'm from won't even look at a Black woman just to say hello. They act as if you don't exist, and purposely stare straight ahead when they pass you on the street. It was very discouraging.

"I've had a few White men approach me for dates—some nice ones, too—but I was never interested in dating outside my race. I had given up hope of ever meeting a Black man, so I buried myself in my work. I had joined a Black book club online, and found out about the Black chatrooms. I wasn't planning to meet anyone, I just wanted to talk to some folks outside of my immediate environment. After four months of exchanging e-mail and telephone conversations, Rodney wanted to meet [me] in person. When he asked, 'Should I come to you, or would you want to come to me?' I got a little panicky."

SIS, IF THE SOIL ON YOUR TURF IS ALL DRIED UP, DON'T HESITATE TO MOVE ON TO GREENER PASTURES

"I definitely didn't want him to meet me in Minneapolis with the dismal conditions surrounding Black relationships—they were basically nonexistent!" exclaimed Karla. "We had spoken about it, but I didn't want him to be scared off by seeing this unfortunate situation face-to-face. But the thought of getting on a plane and flying to another state to meet a man I had never laid eyes on was a little frightening. For some reason, we had never swapped pictures with each other, and all of a sudden I was beginning to wonder if a Black man would really be attracted to me for a serious relationship. This may sound strange to you, but I have never been approached by a Black man wanting a decent relationship. But then I remembered that Rodney wasn't just any man. He was different and special. I felt a kinship with him and could talk with him about anything. We felt comfortable with each other.

"I prayed about it, and I decided to take the chance because we really enjoyed talking with each other so much," Karla continued. "We were developing deep feelings through our correspondence. So I flung my fear out the door and started packing. My family and friends thought I had lost my mind to even entertain the thought of getting on a plane to travel southeast to meet a Black man whom I had only been acquainted with through e-mail and phone calls. 'Do not go to his home. Make sure you stay in a hotel. What if he's a pervert, a lunatic, or a murderer?' they cautioned.

"I understood their fears and concerns, but I really felt I knew him," said Karla. "We had shared so much about ourselves with each other over the months. I was ready for the next step. Two weeks later, I was headed for Norfolk. My grandmother was the only one who sent me off with her blessings. She knew how much he meant to me. 'You are a beautiful young woman, and you deserve a nice young man,' she advised. 'None are here. Take the chance and go meet him. I'm old now, but if I was your age again, I would do exactly what you're doing. Always remember to pray to God to guide your steps. If this young man has any brothers, you can bring some back for some of your cousins and girlfriends.'"

THE GRASS IS INDEED GREENER FOR SISTAS
ON THE OUTSIDE OF MINNEAPOLIS!

"With her [Grandma's] blessings, I boarded the plane," said Karla. "When the plane landed, I didn't need to go to baggage check because all I carried was a weekend bag. As I was walking toward the information desk on the lower level where he had instructed me to meet him, I saw the most handsome and lovely Black man standing there in military uniform. My heart leaped with excitement. His eyes sparkled when he saw me approaching him. He ran toward me, hugged me, smiled, and looked at me deeply and joyfully, as he whispered, 'My angel, welcome to your new home.'

"We both knew from that moment on, he was right," giggled Karla. "His home became my new home. He was a perfect gentleman all weekend. He gave me my own room; we didn't have sex. But we ended up cuddling next to each other in the same bed all weekend. We were married seven months later. Next month will be our nine-year anniversary and the seventh birthday of our second child."

At thirty-six years old today, Karla says she is enjoying a very happy and healthy love connection with her very own loving Black husband. She is enjoying her new hometown and renewed life as a wife, mother, and kindergarten teacher. She said she was able to find her soul mate and Black knight in shining armor because she mustered up the courage and took a step outside of her demographical area. She is also happy to report that she followed her grandmother's advice and has helped five of her sister-friends to "escape from their barren dating life in Minneapolis and to relocate to the greener pastures of Norfolk, a land overflowing with beautiful, single, and available Black brothers."

ZALANDA: BE WILLING TO CLEAR OUT THE EMOTIONAL TRENCHES TOGETHER

Forty-two-year-old Zalanda, a social worker, had a rocky beginning for the first three years of her thirteen-year marriage to forty-one-year-old Kenneth, a city bus driver in Detroit, Michigan. However, she was happy to share that for the past ten years, they have been enjoying matrimonial bliss, and are the proud parents of four well-rounded kids, ages twelve, eleven, six, and four. Zalanda believes that if she and her husband had gotten intensive therapy before tying the knot, they would have been able to prevent many of the abusive and painful experiences they caused each other at the onset of their union.

"Be certain to heal the pains of the past from childhood before starting a family of your own," she warns. "Make sure you check the family background of your husband-to-be also. Two dysfunctional people with a history of emotional, mental, and physical abuse add up to two confused adults getting together to make an even bigger dysfunctional mess. Both of you should first sit down separately, and then together with qualified therapists and marriage counselors to dig deep down in the ditches and get all the dirt out in the open."

Zalanda gives great advice because she is speaking from her past experience. She is a survivor of incest and domestic abuse. "I was molested by an older cousin at a very young age," she confided. "And I had to work through a lot of sexual issues before I could have a normal or good sexual relationship with my husband. I always hated sex in the past, and would try my best to avoid it in my old relationships. But when I turned twenty-two, I graduated from college and became very promiscuous, and I began to use my sexuality as a weapon to control men and get what I wanted from them. I continued to do this until I bottomed out at twenty-six. One day, I took a good look at myself in the mirror, and I didn't like what I saw. I didn't know the stranger who was staring back at me. I was losing myself. I had to change to save my life—so I stopped. I just stopped cold turkey and kept to myself. I was celibate for two whole years. And it felt good. Then one day I met Kenneth in the paper-towel section of a supermarket. We just struck up a conversation and spent half an hour debating over which brand gave you more value for your money. It was so funny."

A NEW BEGINNING STARTS WITH A NEW OUTLOOK

"He made me laugh," Zalanda continued. "As he kept talking, I kept thinking, 'He's not that great-looking, but he's a nice guy.' We headed toward the same cashier and carried on our conversation while waiting on line. He offered to take my bags to the car. I accepted, and we exchanged numbers. He called me that same evening. Our phone calls became a daily ritual. As we got to know each other better, he shared that his father was a heavy drinker and used to beat his mother. He swore that he would never hit a woman, or become an alcoholic. However, he said that he liked to drink a little red wine to unwind from his daily stresses. We formed a bond based on our wounded past. We promised to watch out for each other's back, and to become each other's best friend. And we did.

"We got married at the county clerk's office by the justice of the peace the following year," said Zalanda. "That's when all the demons seemed to rise up out of our pasts to haunt us. I didn't live with him before, so I didn't know that what he referred to as a 'little red wine' meant an entire bottle each day. He didn't know that I sometimes experienced nightmares of being suffocated, and had a hard time breathing during those bouts. The first year and a half of our marriage we stopped laughing together. I only had sex to please him. I hated it, I hated my body, and many times I hated him, too. We were headed for either disaster or divorce court. But the turning point came six months after the birth of our first child. One evening he was so drunk that when he went to pick her up from her crib, he dropped her. She screamed at the top of [her] lungs. I was scared and started screaming, too. When he realized what [had] happened, he fell to his knees, cried like a baby, and asked God to make her be okay, and to forgive and change him. That's when we both entered personal and marriage counseling, and started going to church."

"BEHIND EVERY DARK CLOUD, THERE'S ALWAYS A SILVER LINING"

"Thank God no damage was done to our daughter, but it triggered a new beginning in our lives," recalled Zalanda. "It wasn't easy going through the counseling sessions, but we were both willing to change for each other. Our lives and our family depended on it. For eighteen months we stuck to it, even on the days when we didn't feel like going. We got a sign from our local church and taped it on our refrigerator, 'The Family That Prays Together, Stays Together.'

"We have surely learned how to pray together," Zalanda said, and smiled. "And we are surely blessed. Kenneth and I love each other, we love the Lord, we love our children, and we love life. Thank God we were able to exorcise our past demons from our lives. We brought back laughter into our marriage. Looking at us today, you would never know that a decade ago, we passed through hell and lived to tell about it. We are both on the PTA boards at our children's schools, and Kenneth is the president of our neighborhood community watch. I no longer have nightmares. These days all I have are pleasant dreams of waking up every day to a loving, kind, smart, and considerate man whom I love with all my heart."

What a blessing indeed, sis! May God continue to bless you and your family, with many, many more years of happiness, love, and laughter together. Yours is a fine example of how even the most challenging Black marriages can withstand ugly circumstances, and blossom into beautiful life experiences with proper guidance, prayer, patience, and the willingness of both people to make it work.

ARLENE: SOMETIMES YOU HAVE TO GET ADJUSTED TO A PACKAGE DEAL

When thirty-four-year-old Arlene said yes to thirty-nine-year-old Milton's proposal, little did the unsuspecting sister know that she was not only marrying the man whom she had been in love with for sixteen months, three weeks, and a day before he gathered enough courage to ask for her hand in marriage, but she was also marrying into a ready-made family.

Arlene, an Atlanta photojournalist, met Milton, a mortgage broker, at a self-service gas pump on a sunny Saturday afternoon. He complimented her on her pretty smile, and she returned the kind gesture by paying tribute to his cute dimples. They exchanged business cards, and two weeks later they had their first official date. It was instant combustion, and they felt magnetically attracted to each other. They have been happily bonded and virtually inseparable since their wedding day fourteen years ago.

"Our wedding was just perfect," said Arlene. "But for a while there, it almost never took place. When Milton initially asked me for my hand in marriage, I agreed right away. He had been divorced for three years, and had a high alimony and child-support bill to pay every month. He left the house [to] his ex-wife in Houston, Texas, who was raising their fourteen-year-old son and sixteen-year-old daughter. He was living in a condo in Atlanta, and to save money for our wedding, we agreed to sell my loft and move in together into his smaller two-bedroom apartment."

YOU'VE GOT TO FIGURE OUT WHERE THE KIDS FIT IN

"Eight weeks after we nestled in together, his daughter, Gabrice, decided she wanted to be with her dad and relocate to Atlanta," reported Arlene. "Well, she was the apple of his eye, and he was not one of the stereotypical deadbeat dads. He was a very responsible Black man. His love for his children was one of the characteristics that drew me to him. It was comforting and reassuring to know that when we had children of our own, they would never be abandoned by their father. But being an instant stepmom to a sixteen-year-old was not my idea of beginning on the right foot.

"I was very much in love with Milton and wanted to spend the rest of my life with him. But with moving in so soon, and the immediate extended family, this was too overwhelming for me. I had already sold my apartment, and I really felt cornered. I remembered crying one night and asking God what had I gotten myself into. After a good cry and prayer session, I decided to give it a try and see how things would work out with Gabrice around.

"The first month was a major testing period. I felt like running and leaving everything behind," Arlene admitted. "There were so many things going on at one time. There were four relationships trying to come together under one roof: (1) There was Milton and I trying to get to know each other; (2) Milton and Gabrice's father-and-daughter [bonding]; (3) Gabrice and I were trying to figure out where we stood with each other; and (4) all of us were trying to live together as a family.

"I would caution sisters who are considering marrying a divorced man with children to make sure they first work out all the details and don't assume that they won't be expected to take on some of the parenting responsibilities as well,"

Arlene advised. "I had to sit down and write out my thoughts in a journal. That really helped to save our relationship. I made a list of all the qualities I love and admire about Milton—integrity, responsibility, kindness, honor (and gorgeous dimples)—and I realized that he was demonstrating the qualities that I wanted in my mate. So I had to really take a look at myself and my personal motives."

SEE CHILDREN AS AN EXTENSION OF THEIR PARENT, NOT AS AN INTRUSION ON THEIR PARENT

"Lucky for me, Gabrice was not the kind of kid that competed for her father's attention," Arlene continued. "When I let my guard down, I realized that she just wanted to be loved, by any parent who was willing to guide her through her turbulent teenage stage. Her mother had a new boyfriend who would sleep over at least three times a week, and it caused a rift in their relationship. And her dad had me. She felt alone. I learned to love her as my own. I had to change my perception and look at her as an extension of her father, instead of an intrusion on her father. So I decided to extend a portion of the love I had for Milton to his offspring. Pretty soon, we were all getting along really well. She helped me to plan the wedding and was one of my bridesmaids.

"What I learned through all of this," said Arlene, "is communication is very important. Milton and I talked about everything after that. We decided that he would do all the discipline regarding his children, and would handle all the problems and phone calls from his ex-wife. I left those duties to him, but I was always there for him to talk with and to lean on my shoulder. The next year Gabrice went away to college, but she always came home during her breaks. Two years later, I gave birth to twin boys. Milton was thrilled, and Gabrice is an excellent big sister. We have bought a much bigger home, and we have a great relationship. Gabrice is his only daughter, and she will always have a special place in my heart because she is a beautiful part of the man who I love. And that makes him love me even more."

JACKIE: DON'T GIVE UP ON LOVE WHILE YOU'RE STILL IN THE PRIME OF YOUR LIFE

Forty-five-year-old Jackie says today she can look back at her life six years ago and thank God that she has made it through the "worst life has to offer." She also gives thanks to her thirty-five-year-old husband, Phillip, who she said rescued her from a dead-end path and taught her the meaning of true love.

Two years before Phillip entered her life and as her thirty-seventh birthday approached, Jackie found herself out of work, out of shape, and out of a marriage to an abusive husband who demanded she stay home, collect welfare, cook, clean, take care of their four children, and perform sexual favors at his every command. She described her first husband, forty-eight-year-old Glenroy, as an angry Black man who carried a large chip on his shoulder. They were married when she was twenty-four and he was twenty-seven. He had been in and out of jail for domestic violence on several occasions. She wanted to get away from him but felt there was no way out. It wasn't until Glenroy's first wife, whom he wedded when he was twenty-five in Chicago, was able to finally track him down in Philadelphia that Jackie was truly free from his abuse. When he married Jackie, he neglected to tell her that he was already married; separated but not divorced from his first wife, whom he had left behind with two small children.

Jackie was both relieved and hurt to find out that her twelve-and-a-half-year marriage to a man whom she hated and feared was illegal, and had no value. He was placed in jail, and she was free. At first, she was confused and dismayed, but she wasted no time leaving Philadelphia with her four children and relocating to South Carolina in the home of an older aunt, Alice, who had told her that her home would always be open to Jackie.

IT REALLY IS NEVER TOO LATE TO RENEW THE REAL YOU!

Aunt Alice had no children, so she treated Jackie's four as her very own. She was happy for the company and loved them dearly. The children were happy for the change and adjusted well to their new surroundings. Jackie spent an entire year trying to figure out who she was and what she wanted from life. She used this time to build her self-worth. By her thirty-eighth birthday, she had come full circle and was truly ready to enjoy a life of freedom for the first time ever.

"That's when Phillip entered from nowhere," she recalled. "He owned a good landscaping business with three employees, and would cut and maintain the lawns of all the homes in the area. Every two weeks he would come by; I would be sitting on the porch reading any self-help book I could get my hands on. He was very well-read, and would always suggest some titles that he thought I would be interested in. After a while, he started bringing books for me. I thought that was so sweet and began to notice that he was just as nice-looking on the outside as he was nice on the inside. I wasn't looking for a relationship because I had been through so much, and because he was younger than me, I never thought about him as a potential mate.

"When he asked if I'd like to go out with him sometime, I flatly refused him," she continued. "I told him all about my false husband, and when I started crying, he cried also. I couldn't believe it. I didn't know Black men like this existed. I was used to rough treatment, and here was a man—a younger man—who was respecting my feelings and caring about me. He was nicer and smarter than any of the men I had heard about in my age group. I looked up and saw Aunt Alice staring at us. All she did was smile and nod in approval."

YES SIS, YOU CAN LIVE "HAPPILY EVER AFTER!"

"We started dating that same evening, and were legally married six months later. I just love him, and so do my kids. Our age difference is not an issue for either of us, but you really can't tell that I'm ten years older that him, because in spite of all I've been through, I look younger than my age. But even if I didn't, I really don't care. For the first time in my life, I'm *really* happy and I'm not giving this up. Even though our new family has moved into our own home, the kids still spend weekends with Aunt Alice, who lives only fifteen minutes away. Phillip and I enjoy each other very much, and I just found out that I am six weeks pregnant. We are going to have our own baby!

"Thank God I didn't let his age keep me from seeing what a good, kind, and loving man he is. I had given up on love and marriage until he came into my life. I never knew it was possible to be this happy. Thank you, God!"

NO NEED TO FEAR—LOVE IS VERY NEAR!

I love these stories. These candid revelations certainly prove that there are a lot of Black women enjoying happy and healthy marriages. Sis, isn't it refreshing to hear these good tidings? And isn't it inspirational to receive words of wisdom from women like us who are making it work? While conducting the interviews with these happily married sisters, I was curious to find out if their counterparts felt just as optimistic about enjoying marriage and long-term relationships, so I asked educator Gilbert Lane to share some of the main ingredients needed for longevity in marriage. He should know. He is a decent Black man who is happily married and enjoying healthy love with a dynamic Black woman. He and his wife have successfully made it past their silver anniversary and are looking forward to the gold.

GILBERT: PRESCRIPTIONS FROM A BROTHER IN THE MIX WHO STOOD STEADFAST TO MAKE LOVE LAST

Dr. Grace: Gil, you and your wife, Norma, whom I have had the pleasure of knowing for more than five years now, have recently celebrated your thirtieth wedding anniversary. Wow! First of all, congratulations! With the divorce rate as high as it is today, it is both remarkable and refreshing to speak with someone—a decent man, in fact—who has been successfully married to one woman for this length of time. This is great! Can you give some insight as to how couples can hold a marriage or a love relationship together?

Gilbert: Dr. Grace, longevity in marriage is determined by a sincere commitment to the words "what God has joined together, let no man put asunder." My wife, Norma, and I viewed marriage as more than just a religious ceremony. We looked at it as a sacrament that can never be undone. We both believed that our marriage commitment and vows were not just to each other, but to God. Every marriage will encounter problems—problems that may seem insurmountable, but unless you consider divorce unacceptable, even as a final solution, your marriage may not endure.

REAL ROMANCE IS NOT JUST PHYSICAL, BUT ALSO A DEEP EMOTIONAL EXPRESSION

Dr. Grace: A lot of women (and men) believe that the butterflies-in-the-belly kind of romance should not fade when you get married, but how much of that is really true?

Gilbert: I believe that romance and love are inseparable. Romance is not only sexual. It is the fiber that makes your spouse your best friend. To have romance in your marriage, you don't always have to feel "butterflies in your belly." It can be feeling eager to share something significant with your spouse. It can be the comfort you receive when you don't feel well and your spouse is there to soothe you. I believe that real romance is the emotional and physical bond between you and your spouse that permits you to feel free with each other and enables you to express your love for each other in deep ways that transcend mere sexuality, which is many times fleeting.

Dr. Grace: What are some of love's difficult tests, and how can we overcome them?

Gilbert: I believe the most difficult test in love and marriage is adhering to your commitment to each other; not taking the easy way out. It's important to seek out a mate who has the same belief system that you have; namely, that you both

elationship is everlasting. In order to have such
you both must believe in the saying "To err is
to forgive divine."

My philosophy concerning relationships can be summed
up in dialogue from the movie *A Raisin in the Sun.* To para-
phrase: When do you love someone? When everything is
going right, or when that person is at his lowest?

I believe that the true test of love is how we react when
everything is going wrong and how you and your spouse feel
when your world is coming apart. Anyone can love you when
everything is going great. You must always support each other
regardless of the circumstances. If you have faith and trust in
each other, you will be able to endure any test that life offers.

TO GET TO KNOW YOUR SOUL MATE, YOU HAVE TO USE YOUR HEAD, YOUR HEART, AND YOUR INTUITION

Dr. Grace: From a man's point of view, how do you know
when you've met the ideal mate?

Gilbert: Even though each individual may be different, we do
have something in common: our humanity and free will. We
can, to a certain degree, control our human condition with
respect to selecting a mate. A soul mate has to be not just your
lover or spouse, but your best friend—a person highly
respected and who respects you. Above all, you must take the
time to get to know the person, especially if you would like to
spend the rest of your life with [him or her].

Give yourself the time to interact with your partner in as
many life situations as possible. You must look for telltale positive and negative signs that will guide you in your final selection. Remember, marriage is the most important decision we

have to make; common sense and intuition can be helpful guides.

Dr. Grace: What words of wisdom can you provide about the mate-selection process?

Gilbert: Perhaps the most reliable indicator is common sense. Observing the actions of the person can tell us a great deal. If someone is violent, possessive, unkind, inconsiderate, not trustworthy, irrational, or shows any other signs of instability, these are warning signs. A good man will treat a woman with the respect and love he would show his mother or sister. You can tell a lot by his general attitude toward women. Make sure he treats you with equality, dignity, respect, and love. Don't just follow your heart, follow your head.

Dr. Grace: That's right—the heart plays a major part, but when it's time to wed, we've got to use the head!

A SUPPORTIVE SIS CAN HELP YOU FIND MATRIMONIAL BLISS

I certainly appreciate and respect Gil's advice. I believe it's of great value for us to hear from a brother who loves being married to his sista–soul mate. Still, nothing can compare to the support and encouragement we can get from sister-friends who are already walking on the path that we seek to travel. It is important to surround yourself with positive girlfriends and role models. You may have a female friend who can help you to find healthy love by introducing you to one of her cousins, brothers, uncles, or coworkers, and you could do the same for her. Keep your options open because you never know which door your soul mate will walk through. Remember, mine came through a friend when I least expected it.

I'm not going to ignore the fact that a lot of sisters do not trust other sisters. I know about a lot of the horrendous stories that have happened in the past and I have written about them. Yet I'm not referring to any of the false friendships that our intuition always warns us about. I'm talking about good, genuine friendships filled with positive vibes from healthy-minded sisters—sisters who are looking out for your best interests. It's essential for Black women to have healthy acquaintances with girlfriends and female relatives because it teaches us about *friendship, trust, kindness, respect, patience,* and *communication.* These are the very components that prepare us to find confirmation in healthy love relationships with an ideal mate.

AVOID THE NEGATIVE EMOTIONS THAT CORRUPT HEALTHY DEVOTION

Also, please distance yourself from social circles where the main topic is how "you can't trust any man completely." *Whatever you think is what you attract in your life.* Here's a personal example: I had a very close friend who was so scared and scarred by a divorce she went through fifteen years ago that even today she is very strongly opinioned that "men are not to be trusted." Over the past ten years, I've seen her in two relationships with two wonderful men who loved her very much. However, because of her fear and negative beliefs, she actually created a wedge in each of those relationships. Today, she regrets that she never married either of the two beaus but still refuses to empty out her emotional baggage. Until she does, she will not enjoy a fulfilling relationship with a good man. Here's what's particularly defeating: She has a small group of acquaintances who all share her negative belief, are die-hard defenders of it, and are miserable in their personal lives. Guess what, sis: If you don't believe that you can have healthy love, then you won't. At some point we have to recondition ourselves and let go of past hurts and ill feelings in order to move on and attract enjoyable love.

I like my friend as a person, but I do not like her views on relationships, so I make it a point not to discuss the matter with her or her group of friends. When she is ready to let go of the past, I will be there with open arms and an open heart to help her through the transition so that she may also find the healthy love that is available for her.

THANK GOODNESS FOR GIRLFRIENDS WHO ARE NOT AFRAID OF DELIGHTFUL DREAMS!

While I was writing this section, I had to stop to call my good friend Rayniece to thank her for renewing my hope in marriage. Although we were both single, career-driven women at the time, for the past six years that I'd known her, she always painted a beautiful picture of a future marriage with a fantastic husband. She made it sound so remarkable and possible that you couldn't help but want to get married to your very own soul mate.

Another friend of mine, Maya, and one of my favorite cousins, Connie, were also major influences in shaping my thoughts of the possibility and reality of healthy love. These two women were (and still are) very happily married to wonderful Black men who love them dearly. We were very close, and I was so happy for them that they, in turn, kept cheering me on and inspiring me to "get married to a good man." Once I decided I wanted to get married, I reprogrammed my own thinking and lifestyle with the exercises I shared with you in the first six steps of this book. And it worked! Thank goodness for great advice and support from good girlfriends! Sis, separate from negative influences and surround yourself with positive sister-friends who will cheer you on on your path to healthy love.

HAPPY DESCRIPTIONS WILL REMOVE
UNHEALTHY RESTRICTIONS

Once I had been given encouraging examples of marital bliss and personal assurance, I knew I was ready to get married, form a loving companionship, and create happy memories with an ideal man, but at the time I didn't know who my soul mate was. Although I felt content with my life and accomplishments, I felt an inner spiritual yearning to connect with a more nurturing, higher level of healthy love. The more I prayed about it, the more I found myself drawn into acquaintances with women who were happily married to their soul mates. You know the old wise adage "When the student is ready, the teacher will appear"? Sis, I was ready. I was curious and wanted to know how it felt to be married to a compatible mate, and how to make it last once you've linked with him. These women became my teachers, and I was their student. I was very inspired by their testimonies, and it is with great joy that I share the highlights of their checklist for long-lasting love with you.

Seven Quick Tips for Loving Good
Directly from the Sistahood
  1. Talk things out.
  2. Share similar interests and values.
  3. Set aside some private time for yourself.
  4. Be yourself.
  5. Be each other's best friend.

6. Be sincere and up-front.
7. Learn to laugh together.

THE GOAL IS NOT JUST THE LEGAL PACT BUT MORE IMPORTANT THE SACRED CONTRACT

My first guest-expert appearance on the TV talk show *Men Are from Mars, Women Are from Venus* was on a special program designed for an all-male audience. The topic was "Everything You Always Wanted to Know About Women, but Were Afraid to Ask." My advice about making relationships last beyond the wedding received so much admiration and applause from both the audience and the host that the producer invited me back for two additional tapings.

Here is the summation of my commentary in a nutshell: The thing to keep in mind most of all is the sanctity of marriage. More important than the wedding ceremony, rings, photo albums, marriage license, or any other physical contract is the sacred emotional contract you and your partner make with each other. You are not *truly* soul mates just because you've signed all the binding legal documents, or just because everyone thinks you are. Sis, you are *truly* soul mates because the two of you have intertwined spiritually, mentally, emotionally, and physically. You have both agreed to spend every moment of your lives together, not just one day to celebrate a wedding and exchange rings.

I really like the beautiful diamond engagement ring Richard gave me when he proposed, but in comparison to the emotional commitments he made and has honored thus far, the ring will never compare. It was his sealed emotional contract of deep love, respect, kindness, and promise of monogamy that makes me confident that I have married my very own soul mate. You will feel that way, too, very soon.

YOU DESERVE HEALTHY LOVE, SIS!

Now that you've traveled through the seven steps of how to get the healthy love you want and deserve, let me ask you a small variation of the important question I asked you at the beginning of this guidebook. How does it feel to *know* that there is someone out there to love you just for who you are?

Take a deep breath, sis. . . . Clear your mind. . . . Close your eyes for a moment, and think about this: What is it like to *know* that your very own soul mate is waiting to enjoy a healthy love relationship and marriage with you?

It's a nice feeling, isn't it? And it's real! I've shared my personal story with you, and you've read the stories of other sisters just like you who have found their perfect love connection (even though some of them thought it was too late at one point in their lives). It's never too late, sis. I'm living proof of that, and I'm talking to you personally, heart to heart from this page. Maybe you weren't aware that while you were reading this, a powerful and wonderful experience was taking place within you and on your spiritual plane. You were sending out silent prayers, either consciously or subconsciously, to bring "the right one" into your life. The amazing thing is you are already on the path to making this dream materialize on the physical plane.

Can you feel the reality of it? Lift yourself to a higher spiritual level and connect with God, sis. Your Creator did not put you on Earth to be lonely. Being alone at certain times in our lives provides beautiful opportunities to get to know ourselves and grow closer to our Maker. However, when you are sincerely ready, sis—mentally, emotionally, spiritually, and physically—to let your soul mate into your heart and life, it will happen. I promise.

Now let me ask you this: *Are you ready?* If your answer is no, then put this book aside in a safe place where you keep all your important belongings, and come back to it when you are truly ready to experience and enjoy a life-enriching relationship with a fantastic man.

If your answer is yes, then go ahead, sis; do what I did: Ask, believe, receive, accept, and enjoy the healthy love life that you want and *deserve!*

"Therefore I say to you, all things for which you pray and ask, believe that you have received them, and you shall have them."

Mark 11:24

■ about the author

Dr. Grace Cornish is a spiritual psychologist, television personality, motivational speaker, leader of sold-out seminars, and the award-winning author of three enormously popular books. She is known to millions of television viewers from her frequent appearances as the resident "after-care" psychologist on the *Queen Latifah Show* and from her appearances on *Good Day New York, Ricki Lake, Oh Drama!, Ananda Lewis,* and the *Montel Williams* shows. Dr. Grace's advice is always down-to-earth and highly effective, and has landed her on FOX-TV, WOR-TV, NBC, CBS, ABC, and BET programs.

She is a widely sought-after keynote speaker and seminar leader who ministers not only to people's minds, but also to their spirits. Her talks about making God accessible are extremely effective in helping women (and men) from all walks of life. She has a Ph.D. in social psychology and a masters (MPS) in urban ministry, and is frequently quoted in *Essence, Ebony, Jet, Black Elegance, Upscale, Honey, Heart & Soul,* and *Today's Black Woman.*

Publishers Weekly said of her most recent book, *10 Good Choices That Empower Black Women's Lives,* "An author who clearly knows her audience, Cornish provides warm, sister-to-sister explanations that are personal yet universal, and will help steer women toward better lives, with a firm and loving hand. . . . one of the biggest black woman's self-help books of the season, and a great choice for reading groups."

Her familiar title, *10 Bad Choices That Ruin Black Women's Lives,* has been on the *Essence* and *Blackboard* national best-seller lists several times, and is a favorite in Doubleday's *Black Expression* book club. Dr. Grace has been interviewed numerous times on BBC radio about her international bestseller *Radiant Women of Color.*

In the course of her career, she has received a number of honors and outstanding awards, including recognition by *Who's Who in America, Who's Who in the East,* and *Who's Who in Writers, Editors, and Poets.* Dr. Grace has also been the recipient of many excellent reviews.

For further information or to contact Dr. Grace for book signings or speaking engagements, you can visit her website: www.drcornish.com.